Zen Between Two Bicycle Wheels: Eat, Pedal, Sleep

BABY BOOMERS BICYCLING AMERICA'S WEST COAST

FROSTY WOOLDRIDGE

authorHOUSE

AuthorHouse™
1663 Liberty Drive
Bloomington, IN 47403
www.authorhouse.com
Phone: 1 (800) 839-8640

Published by AuthorHouse   05/21/2020

ISBN: 978-1-7283-6250-2 (sc)
ISBN: 978-1-7283-6249-6 (e)

Library of Congress Control Number: 2020909394

Print information available on the last page.

Any people depicted in stock imagery provided by Getty Images are models, and such images are being used for illustrative purposes only. Certain stock imagery © Getty Images.

This book is printed on acid-free paper.

To

Gary and Marty North for their wisdom, leadership and guidance through my college years. They brought me stability, integrity and hope in the 1960's when the world spun into confusion, anger and conflict. May their impact on the world and all the lives they inspired be a beacon for everyone on this planet.

The Energy, The Ecstasy, And The Courage Of Your Journey

A blank spot on the map dances with your imagination. What treasures might it hold? As you swing your leg over the top tube, your touring bike allows you unlimited freedom of flight for your body, mind and spirit. Slip your hands into your riding gloves. Grab those handlebars. Press your feet onto the pedals. Click the brake handles. Slide your derriere onto the saddle. Look toward the distant horizon that beckons your dreams. Feel the energy coursing through your body. Make that first pedal stroke downward as your thighs lift you onto adventure highway. Time means nothing now. It slips away as easily as grains of sand on a wind-swept beach. But those grains only trade places. On your bike, you move into that blank spot—new locations in the passage of time. The pedaling becomes incidental—like breathing. The hills and mountains come and go—your legs powering over them in a kind of winsome trance. Grappling with headwinds brings determination; while riding a tailwind fetches ecstasy. Rain drenches you during a bicycle adventure, yet promises a rainbow. Bicycle touring demands you dig deep into the art of living. Each challenge lets you know you're vibrantly alive. You transform into a state of bliss, much like an eagle gliding over majestic mountains. You see them soaring, just living. You soar with them as you glide down a mountain grade. Those moments present you with uncommon experiences that give your life eternal expectation. That's bicycle adventure! FHW

Your Adventure, Your Journey, Your Zen

If you're reading this story, you might be a baby boomer. Born between 1946 and 1964, over 80 million of you hopped onto planet Earth for a ride on the wild side. Your dads returned home from WWII with quiet demeanors. You grew up with Howdy Doody and Captain Kangaroo. Roy Rogers and Dale Evans saved us from the bad guys. Doris Day sang and Rachel Welsh entertained. John Wayne, Steve McQueen and Yul Brenner topped the movie charts. Fess Parker played Daniel Boone.

You lived through those "Happy Days" for real as you cruised the Dairy Queen parking lot looking at the babes or stud-muffins from your high school. Upon entering college, you demonstrated against the Vietnam War. "Hell no, we won't go…." You remember Woodstock. You served in the military. You watched in stunned amazement at the movie "Easy Rider" with Peter Fonda and Dennis Hopper. "The Graduate" with Dustin Hoffman taught you that all wasn't as it seemed in the adult world.

Elvis Presley remained the "King of Rock n' Roll", Jim Morrison sang "Come on baby light my fire…", Jimi Hendricks strummed his guitar, and Mick Jagger with the Rolling Stones sang, "Can't get no satisfaction…." You may have smoked some dope. You probably "inhaled" much like Bill Clinton didn't. The Beatles took America by storm with, "She loves you, ya, ya, ya….and Sergeant Pepper's Lonely Hearts Club Band."

On the country music side, you admired Johnny Cash, Waylon Jennings, Dolly Parton, Reba McEntire, Bonnie Raitt and Willie Nelson. You loved listening over and over to Willie's, "On the road again…can't wait to get back on the road again…."

Whether you stumbled out of high school or attended college, you saw the world as a wide-open adventure. You explored Europe on a Eurail Pass. You got stoned or tried cocaine, maybe some "schrooms." College coeds tossed their bras and women's liberation became the sign of the times. Peace rings, tie-dyed T-shirts and peace flags popped up everywhere.

Additionally, racial conflict erupted with Dr. Martin Luther King marching from Montgomery to Selma, Alabama. Detroit rioted and all hell broke loose when King suffered assassination.

If you graduated from high school, you may have traveled in a van around the USA or motorcycled with buddies. You stumbled into your first job. If you attended college, you enjoyed four years of learning that also kept you out of the draft. You may have been conscripted into the U.S. Army ending up in 11 Bravo—Infantry. You witnessed some really ugly situations in Vietnam and/or became disillusioned with politics, especially LBJ and Tricky Dick. You discovered that our U.S. government and our leaders lie like a den of thieves.

Several years later, you met and married your lady or your handsome man in shining armor. You tried several jobs until you found one that met your financial needs. Before you knew it, the stork graced you with a beautiful newborn. In a blink, that white-winged bird brought another bundle of joy.

From there, you faced 25 years of bills from mortgage, car payments, groceries, dental, car insurance, life insurance and money for their college expenses. Around 50, those precious kids became adults, and in an instant, they left the nest.

You took up cycling with clubs because you found a sense of freedom from cranking the pedals. Interestingly, you subscribed to Adventure Cycling Magazine to see retired Americans over 65 bicycling coast-to-coast or riding from the Canadian Border to the Mexican Border. Many traveled across Canada from Vancouver, British Columbia to St. Johns, Newfoundland, or the Lewis & Clark Trail from Astoria, Oregon to St. Louis, Missouri. Others took "Bike and Barge" trips throughout Europe or other guided trips to Alaska.

Their stories excited something in the far reaches of your youth. "If those couples are riding all over the place, why can't we ride?" you ask your spouse.

You might be reminded of James T. Kirk in the original Star Trek series of the mid-60's when the good captain and Mr. Spock raced all over the universe at Warp Factor Nine. Those adventures excited your imagination. Later, Captain Jean Luc Picard of the Starship Enterprise said it best, "Someone once told me that 'time' was a predator that stalks us all our lives. I rather believe that time is a companion that goes with us on a journey. It reminds us to cherish each moment, because it will never come again. What we leave behind is not as important as how we lived."

That last sentence says it all, "What we leave behind is not as important as how we lived."

So, what kind of adventures cause you great excitement? If it's pedaling a bicycle, you hit the jackpot. From my 15 bicycle adventures across America and the experiences gained, in 2017, I guided four guys from 65 to 72 across the Northern Tier of America from Astoria, Oregon to Bar Harbor, Maine—4,100 miles. That resulted in the book: **Old Men Bicycling Across America: A Journey Beyond Old Age.**

Within a week, two of the rookies, both 70, who had never ridden more than day-rides, stepped up to me, "Frosty, this is the greatest adventure of my life! And, it's just starting. I can't thank you enough for taking me with you. I don't think I had the courage to try it myself."

In 2018, Sandi and I decided to ride the West Coast from Blaine, Washington on the Canadian border to Tijuana, Mexico. It's known as the fabled West Coast Bicycle Tour on Route 101—one of the most delightful cycle rides in North America. It's the most entertaining, the most historical and the most spiritual ride I've ever enjoyed. Not to mention the wonder of riding along the Oregon Coast, through the redwoods and Big Sur!

While this might be an inspirational guidebook for baby boomers to ride the West Coast, it's also a story of overcoming the challenges of old age. You might like some suggestions for all the maladies that we both suffer from being in our 70's.

Additionally, Chapter 23 offers you nearly a dozen couples and single senior citizens who overcame tremendous challenges to ride their bikes across America. Some of them lost their spouses several months before their rides. Other couples found creative solutions to overcome their incompatibilities.

If this book inspires you beyond the pages, Chapter 24 offers you everything you need to know about bicycle touring nationally and internationally. You will see E-bikes celebrated in this book because they give individuals or couples a whole new lease on short and/or long-distance cycling adventures.

Please note that bicycle travel carries its own dangers. The safer you ride with a rear-view mirror and with brightly colored jerseys, with flashing lights, and flags you carry on your bike—the better your chances of a glorious finish. While this book encourages, inspires and shows you great places along the coast—you alone assume responsibility for your life and your ride along the West Coast or any tour you might take in the future.

On this journey, relish the highs, endure the lows and savor the in-between times. Pedal into those sunrises that light the sky with promise. Cherish those elegant sunsets with their exclamation point to your incredible day on your bicycle. Remember the good, bad and ugly moments. Stand tall that you possessed the courage to explore the world on your iron steed. It carried you into your dreams where you traveled into those epic moments of awe, wonder and splendor.

Contents

Section III—State of California

Introduction

Your life on a bicycle begins with you in the saddle, pressing your thighs into the pedals, moving into the morning sunshine, sweating in the heat of the day, climbing the next hill and guzzling from your water bottle. Trail mix crunches around your teeth. Cherries, oranges and bananas taste like heaven on earth. A watermelon equates to the divine. Chase and catch the things you love in life. When you follow that path, your best friends appear. Your high-spoke vibrations attract the noblest and brightest along life's highway. Share your dream with another cyclist. Ask about theirs. Get lost in the heat of the day while you pedal into that sweet spot in the afternoon when the air cools to match that flawless moment of perfection your bicycle Zen. Life beckons you to live your dreams and wear your passions with a smile. FHW

Back in the days of your youth, you pedaled a bicycle on a paper route, off to school and/or pedaled with a bunch of friends on back roads, through the woods or just screwed around on a city block.

Riding a bicycle provided fun, freedom and a certain sense of elation for your spirit. For the most part, you took it for granted. It didn't occur to you that a piece of steel, propelled by a chain drive, navigated by handlebars, and complimented with two rubber tires wrapped around metal rims—could carry you around the world.

As kids, you clipped playing cards to your spokes to make noise as if you rode a high-powered bike. Or, maybe you wanted your parents to notice you! You raced each other, cracked wheelies and out-ran neighborhood dogs. Along the way, you crashed, tore your pants and skinned your knuckles.

Somehow, without a helmet on your head, you survived your childhood. Not without a few chipped teeth, stitches, broken bones and bruised muscles!

As time passed, you graduated from high school only to buy a car or motorcycle. Millions of Schwinn bikes hung from the rafters of parents' garages. Some teens left for college, where they rode their bikes to class. But, after four years, they graduated into real life with jobs, cars and marriage.

Their bicycles found new rafters in the garage with plenty of dust dulling the finish over the years.

As for this cyclist, I remember my paper route days back in the 1960's. At first, I walked my 80-customer route. It burned a lot of time. I asked my dad if he would buy me a bicycle.

"If you want a bike," he said. "You earn it. Save up your route money and buy it on lay-away."

After three months, I plunked down $60.00 for a fat-tire Schwinn Wasp. I added some big baskets on the back and the front. It resembled a beast of burden.

From that day forward, I sailed through my route. I got so good that I could throw a folded paper at the door and see it break open, ready to read. I watched lots of deer, rabbits, racoons and skunks in the early morning light. Birds chirped from the branches and waves of geese filled the skies during the spring and autumn migrations. And those sunrises, well, they filled me with visual expectation of the creativity of Mother Nature. What a show!

Of course, dogs found me as easy prey. They chased me, nipped at me, and several tore pieces out of my trousers.

After my route, a hot shower and Wheaties with sliced bananas finished my morning routine. I pedaled off to school. You might say I enjoyed a great childhood. I loved that Schwinn Wasp. It gave me freedom!

After high school, I rode it to classes every day through my college years. During the last week of finals, someone stole it. I cried at the loss of my friend. However, life called, and I joined the U.S. Army. After my service, I moved forward to a teaching job in Colorado.

In the case of this cyclist and many others out of the 60's, the new high-speed Schwinn Continental with 10 speeds, offered a whole new perspective in bicycle travel. I cranked up mountain passes with ease. I flat-out hauled ass on the flats with a flip of the lever.

A friend and I raced each other to work daily. We got up early to bicycle eastbound for 24 miles to work on the arid plains in Brighton, Colorado. We pedaled into glorious sun rises that sprayed the heavens with chameleon clouds and majestic thunderheads. Once at work, we took showers and started our day. After work, we cranked toward the mountains with stunning sunsets expanding the skies with a rainbow of colors. At that point, as a young man in my twenties, I felt the wonder of my bike, yet, I took it for granted.

ON THE EDGE OF WONDER

In the summer of 1974, I rode my motorcycle to Alaska. After crossing the Arctic Circle, I met two guys on bicycles stopped alongside the gravel road. I said, "What are you two doing up here on the Dalton Highway on bicycles?"

"We rode from San Diego, California to reach the Arctic Circle," one said.

"A motorcycle will get you there faster and easier," I said.

"Yeah," he said. "But all you do is turn the throttle and watch the scenery fly by at 60 mph. You miss most of it in one big blur. At 12 miles per hour, the landscape etches memories into your thighs. You live on the edge of wonder every mile."

"On the edge of wonder," I muttered.

"Yup," he said. "On a bicycle tour, you become the adventure."

As I throttled away from those two guys, I ruminated about his comment, "on the edge of wonder" for several days. That single comment played on my mind for the next week. I powered my motorcycle across the Alaskan wilderness, but in that one single comment with two guys exploring on bicycles, my life changed.

Back at school that autumn, I spoke with my riding buddy.

"Ward," I said. "What do you think of me bicycling coast to coast next year, Los Angeles to Jekyll Island, Georgia on the Atlantic?"

"Wish I could go with you," he said. "But my wife won't let me. Heck, you're single, so do it! It will transform you. It will be a thousand times more fun than our morning rides."

"Well, it sounds pretty crazy, but that touring cyclist in Alaska said that I would live on the 'edge of wonder' for the entire journey," I said.

"I've done week-long tours," Ward said. "That pretty much sums it up."

COAST TO COAST

That next spring of 1975, I announced that I planned to bicycle coast-to-coast across America.

"You're crazy," several colleagues said. "You could get run over out there with the drunks or someone swatting their kids instead of keeping their eyes on the road."

Nonetheless, I figured if those two guys could pedal their bikes up to Alaska, I could crank 3,000 miles across America.

"I'm going!" I said.

Perhaps I should have paused when I couldn't get anyone else to accompany me on that first grand bicycle adventure.

"You're nuts, man," friends told me.

Nonetheless, I bought a bike billed as a 'touring bicycle' with racks, panniers, drop bars and mountain gearing.

For equipment, I carried a stove, pot and utensils. I bought rain gear, shorts and shanked shoes to protect my feet from being crushed with constant pedaling. I ordered an excellent helmet. I carried three water bottles. I added long sleeve jerseys and extra underwear. For the most part, I didn't possess any idea about the challenges of bicycle touring. Remember the adage, "You'll learn the hard way."

In June, I took a train out to Los Angeles. Several days later, I dipped the back tire into the Pacific Ocean on Manhattan Beach. On the back of my rear pack, I displayed a sign, "Coast to Coast."

"That should get a little attention," I muttered to myself.

After pushing the bike through 100 yards of sand and plenty of beach people staring at me, I reached the pavement. I hopped onto the bike for a ride through the insane Los Angeles traffic. Almost accidently, I pointed my left hand down to the ground and then, pointed it eastward, like Ward Bond in the TV series of the 60's, "Wagon Train", and yelled, "Forward, Ho!"

After two days of dodging LA traffic and inhaling copious amounts of smog, I reached the Mojave Desert heading toward the Colorado River and Arizona.

A NEW UNDERSTANDING OF HUNGER

Sitting by a campfire one night, I looked up at the stars to see the Big Dipper, Orion and Aquarius. Shooting stars sliced through the ink-black of space to provide an exclamation point to the day's ride. I stirred my Dinty Moore vegetable stew while dipping bread into the broth. For some reason, it tasted better than anything I had ever eaten before.

While devouring vegetable stew, peanuts, bread, tomatoes, avocados, apples, peaches and just about everything else I could get my hands on, I felt a warm sense of satisfaction overwhelm me. The starlight gleamed off my bike metal. My tent and sleeping bag awaited me. In the distance, a coyote howled in the bush. Not to be outdone, a Great Horned Owl hooted through the night air from a nearby tree with a sense of curiosity about this strange being on a bicycle who pitched a tent and built a campfire.

"Damn!" I said. "This is neat stuff. I almost feel like I'm dreaming, but I'm awake and sitting here in the middle of my dream as I stare into the embers of this campfire. This bicycle touring, man, it's pretty cool."

That night transformed me into a long-distance touring bicycle traveler. Since then, I have bicycled 15 times across the United States coast-to-coast and/or Canada to Mexico. I've bicycled and camped across six continents, including parts of Antarctica. It's been one hell of an extraordinary journey of animals, people, amazing sights and epic moments.

At 73 years of age, I don't take anything for granted anymore. Every day I am alive and healthy proves a bonus. I hang with guys who are gray haired, gray bearded, bald and fighting high blood pressure.

JOURNEY BEYOND OLD AGE

If you like to pedal a bicycle or you once loved to ride a bicycle, this book may inspire you. If you're facing old age or stand in the middle of it somewhere between 60 and 80, you're looking out a window that narrows with each daybreak. With that in mind, my wife Sandi, 70, and I decided to ride the West Coast of America.

If this book ignites your imagination, the last two chapters instruct you in everything you need to know on how to start your own bicycle adventure across America.

You're invited to share this journey in words, songs, people and animals. It's the stuff of life. While you're here, charge toward living. Life provides you with this unique moment of adventure.

If the roar of a wave crashes beyond your campsite, you might call that adventure. When coyotes howl outside your tent--that may be adventure. While you're sweating like a horse in a climb over a 12,000-foot pass, that's adventure. When a howling headwind presses your lips against your teeth, you're facing a mighty adventure. If you're pushing through a raging rainstorm, you're drenched in adventure. But that's not what makes an adventure. Instead, it's your willingness to struggle through it, to present yourself at the doorstep of Nature. That creates the experience. No greater joy can come from life than to live inside the moment of an adventure. It may be a momentary high, a stranger that changes your life, an animal that delights you or frightens you, a struggle where you triumphed, or even failed, yet you braved the challenge. Those moments present you uncommon experiences that give your life eternal expectation. That's adventure! FHW

THE CHARACTERS WHO MAKE UP A JOURNEY

On this journey, my wife Sandi rode her new Hai-Bike E-bike. She loves that bike because it allows her to travel with me with ease. She pedals up mountain grades with little effort because the bike possesses four levels of enhanced pedaling.

Sandi said, "I encourage any woman over 60 to buy an E-bike because it allows you to ride easily and efficiently. It's just as much fun as pedaling a regular bike. You can buy some that will give you full assist or partial help. My bike runs for 75 miles on one charge, so it's a blessing to my mind and also my body."

I love this quote: "The bicycle is just as good company as most husbands and, when it gets old and shabby, a woman can dispose of it and get a new one without shocking the entire community." Ann Strong, Minneapolis Tribune, 1895.

Sandi retired as an RN after 35 years working her tailfeathers off. She reared two boys, which she calls, "My greatest gifts."

As for me, after I discharged out of the Army, I started out as a math-science teacher in Brighton, Colorado, north of Denver. The fabulous woman I married out of college turned out to be a five-star hotel-style lady. She loved luxury. I loved camping, skiing and mountain climbing. Amicably, we decided to go our separate ways after three years of incompatibility. She moved forward and married a guy more her style. I stayed single for the next 35 years.

After five years of poverty wages at $5,000.00 a year, I decided to become a writer. I suffered hundreds of rejection slips. It took me 22 years before my first book published. I kept at it and today, I'm nearing 20 published books.

Also, along my life journey, I became a cardiac catheterization medical technician, lifeguard, short order cook, long-haul truck driver for United Van Lines, dance teacher, bartender, personal trainer and safety director for a moving company.

My favorite authors: Louisa May Alcott, John Muir, Jane Goodall, Emerson, Diane Ackerman, T.S. Elliot, Jack London, Richard Bach, Thoreau, Rachel Carson, Eleanor Roosevelt, Robert Heinlein and Edward Abbey. I love this quote by the great author John Steinbeck in his book, **Travels with Charley: In Search of America.**

"Once a journey is designed, equipped, and put in process, a new factor enters and takes over. A trip, a safari, an exploration, is an entity, different from all other journeys. It has personality, temperament, individuality, and uniqueness. A journey is a person in itself; no two are alike. And all plans, safeguards, policing, and coercion are fruitless. We find after years of struggle that we do not take a trip; a trip takes us. Tour masters, schedules, reservations, brass-bound and inevitable, dash themselves to wreckage on the personality of the trip. Only when this is recognized can the blown-in-the glass bum relax and go along with it. "Only then do the frustrations fall away. In this a journey is like marriage. The certain way to be wrong is to think you control it."

Like Steinbeck said, "…we don't take a trip; a trip takes us."

ACHES AND PAINS OF OLD AGE

If you think it's easy riding a bicycle past the age of 70, think again. You've got to deal with bad knees, failing hips, overweight issues, diabetes issues and high blood pressure. You face circulation problems, joint issues, sore feet, and aches and pains in places you never knew existed. Your hands grow numb from pressure on the bars while your elbows and shoulders take a constant pounding from the road. You may endure an enlarged prostate that has you heading to the bathroom too often during the day, and worse, during the night.

Additionally, we all sport gray hair and beards, or bald heads. There's nothing sexy about wrinkles, age spots, dark moles and pot bellies. Our teeth: not as white as in our youths. Skin sagging? Plenty in the baby boomer group.

When we look at ourselves in the mirror, the question jumps out, "How in the hell did I get this old this fast?"

Guess what? There's nothing you can do about it.

While I am lean and in great condition, I suffer from high blood pressure. My dad died of a heart attack at 46. My brother died at 50 of the same. My other brother suffered a stroke at 55. Presently, I follow **The Sinatra Solution** to lower my blood pressure via nutrients. I keep a steady 120/80 most days.

To keep my prostate healthy, I consume daily a dosage of saw palmetto berry, zinc, lycopene, B-6, copper, pygeum and pumpkin seed extract. Other combinations give men a better chance of maintaining a healthy prostate. You may find them in any health-food store.

Another thing that bugs me about getting old: I can't remember things that happened recently. While speaking, I can't find the words to fit into a sentence. I 'search' through my brain to find the word, but if I can't find it, I use another word. It's highly frustrating. It appears to be slow onset dementia. The other day, I saw a poster of Paul Newman in a store. I couldn't remember his name. It took me a full five minutes to wander around my mind until I finally discovered his name. Talk about frustrating! Presently, I take daily pills of Lion's Mane and phosphatidylserine, also known as PS, to keep my brain sharp. It has improved my memory dramatically. I'm not looking forward to what ageing will do to my brain when I reach 80, which, by the way, will arrive in a blink of time.

Additionally, four years ago, my right knee suffered breakdown from an old racquetball injury that kept getting worse. After the 2016 cross country ride, I figured my bicycle days might come to an end. Back in Denver, I heard about "Stem Cell Therapy." I booked an appointment the next week. After taking X-rays, they said my knee would respond with 99 percent healing.

"Your knee will be as good as new," said Dr. Cantor.

"Let's do it," I said.

Dr. Michael Cantor gave a speech on Ted Talks that will give you an idea of the incredible healing power of stem cells. There's another series titled, "The Truth About Stem Cells" by Neil Riordan, Ph.D. https://www.youtube.com/watch?v=f9O3Lyz8qw0

After the procedure where they extracted marrow out of my bones and spun my blood into "platelet rich plasma", they reinjected the stem cells with my 'super blood' back into my knee. Within the next 12 months, my knee healed to the point that I jumped back into the bumps for skiing. I still curried concern over the knee making a 4,100-mile bike trip in 2017. I trained to get my knee ready for tough pedaling in the mountains. After two weeks and countless mountain passes, my knee performed like a teenager. I pedaled 100-mile days or 50-mile days with no pain or freeze-up.

One of my friends on that ride sported 40 pounds of excess weight. He hated being fat. When he wore skintight riding nylons and jerseys, that pot belly stuck out like a sore thumb. His father died of a heart attack at 62, so he rode a delicate line between life and death. He tried to become a vegetarian like me, but he fell back into his voracious appetite and beer habits.

There's something to be said about "eat, drink and be happy, for tomorrow you die." If you're enjoying your life with all your vices, it's your life, and you get to live it at your pleasure.

Another friend on that ride faced high cholesterol which could give him a stroke or heart attack on a mountain pass. For him, he might eat less red meat and dairy products, but, again, there's something to be said like Frank Sinatra, "I did it my way."

One thing can be noted about bicycle touring after age of 60: you regain your health as you engage your body in daily exercise. Your blood flows free, lean and clean. Your fat burns away. You will feel powerful impulses in your muscles as they tune, tone and tighten under your skin. Aches and pains subside. You might want to try a natural pain killer called: curcumin or turmeric. It's all natural and it relieves pain without side-effects. You renew your entire physical makeup by healthy eating of fruits, vegetables, legumes, nuts, salads and ocean-going Atlantic salmon. It's good to take multi-vitamins to ensure that micro-nutrients feed your cells with all the minerals and vitamins they need to operate at peak efficiency.

In the end, we're all here for a short time on this planet, so each of us gets to choose to make it a good time as we define it.

At hiker/biker camp spots, world travelers of every description entertain you with their stories. Or, you might like to motel it down the coast. Or, you may enjoy www.WarmShowers.org hosts the entire journey. Some riders carry not much more than a credit card, energy bars, water and rain suit. Additionally, Air B and B's abound along the route. Look for super hosts that offer the finest in local knowledge, food and sights to see.

Whatever your style, you may inspect the last two chapters of this book for "everything you need to know about long-distance touring."

Safety first: Sandi and I recommend white, orange or fluorescent green helmets, fluorescent green jerseys, eight-foot vertical orange, white and fluorescent flags off your back rack, and an orange, fluorescent flag 20 inches into traffic. Those flags flap all the time to give your location to cars speeding along at 60 miles per hour. Additionally, you can buy red-white USB eight-hour charged blinking lights that really flash into the oncoming rear traffic. You'll see all the safety information and how to install it in the last two chapters.

Once into California, be prepared to marvel as you pedal through

Prairie Creek Redwood Park. Be sure to stop at the "Big Tree." Be prepared to stand aghast at the size of that monster 2,000-year-old redwood. It's a magical 10-mile trip through those ambassadors from the time of the Roman Empire.

Later, you can't pedal slowly enough through the "Avenue of the Giants." Later, stay a day in the logging town of Mendocino made nostalgic by the song in the 1960's. Finally, you reach the Golden Gate Bridge and San Francisco. Stay awhile on Fisherman's Wharf and taste the chocolates. Hire a street artist draw your picture on a big piece of paper. He'll give you a tube to mail it home. It'll become a favorite keep sake.

Out of San Francisco, nothing like Monterrey Bay with John Steinbeck's "Cannery Row" and a 17-mile run through the wealth of Pebble Beach Golf Course and billionaires' mansions. Then, Big Sur awaits you with three days of sensational, stupendous and fantastic bicycling.

After that, the Hearst Castle astounds you with its beauty, audacity and filthy rich money of Mr. William Randolph Hearst, the most spoiled man in all of American history.

The ride continues with excitement of elephant seals and finally, the ride into the fabled beaches along the coast and into Los Angeles. You'll never see so many wild and wacky people as those who inhabit the beaches. And, a stop at the Santa Monica Pier, end of Route 66, promises a great day of sightseeing. Along the way, always keep your eyes on your bikes, and keep them locked up.

In the final days of the ride, you realize your enormous dollops of fun are coming to an end. You pedal through San Diego with the aircraft carrier on display, submarine and sailing ships, dry-docked Queen Elizabeth steamship and the statue of a sailor kissing the nurse to celebrate the end of WWII. Also, a statue of Bob Hope entertaining a group of soldiers, and onto the border where you can "touch" Mexico and take pictures of a sign: entering Mexico.

Admittedly, I love this ride so much, I've completed it four times. For certain, you will remember this "epic" journey for the rest of our life. Hopefully, you took 1,000 pictures, videos and lots of notes for your family and friends. To make it more fun, post on social media to gather and inspire a strong following.

Spectacular Moments on Tour

"The stretch of serpentine highway south of Monterey Bay, California known as the Big Sur, creates a dynamic collision of cliffs and waves of the Pacific Ocean on the West Coast of America. A cyclist sweats while climbing its serpentine ridges. A rider yells with delight while screaming down its raging descents. Cyclists stand with their mouths agape at every vista stop where the ocean collides with the rocky cliffs. At some point, you touch the waves, and at others, you fly 1,000 feet above the surf. All in all, Big Sur etches its grandeur into your thighs while carving memories into your adventure to last a lifetime." FHW

Have you ever awoken one day on your own adventure not imagining what you faced? Have you ever climbed a mountain only to be confronted by a bear? Did you crack out of your tent to see a stunning sunrise? What happened on that canoe trip in January in Michigan on the Pine River when you caught a log and fell into icy waters? I did and froze half to death while contracting pneumonia. You never know what to expect on an adventure. How do you define it?

One thing equates to adventure: it may not always be comfortable, but it's still adventure.

We woke up to birds squawking in the trees and the sound of waves crashing on the beach. Seagulls bickered with one another while pelicans glided over the crest of waves. We stretched, cooked breakfast and pulled up the tent, and packed the gear.

For the entire morning, we cranked up 1,000-foot cliffs only to descend back down to 300 feet. The blue Pacific Ocean waters sparkled like trillions of diamonds. Aspirin-white waves crashed onto sandy beaches.

Every kind of bird flew in every kind of formation. The road resembled a thin snake with no end as it slithered around every contour of the terrain.

At one moment, we traveled through dense woods and just as suddenly, upward along a barren rock cliff. Out in the water, rock islands featured hundreds of seabirds like cormorants, pelicans and sea gulls. Otters slapped their flippers as they floated on their backs. Seals played in the surf.

The stunning scenery around us made the pedaling incidental. It felt like when those kids rode with E.T. across the full moon. A feeling swept over us as if we rode with the "Universe." We pedaled an elegant serpent meandering on the wings of the Pacific Ocean.

The Big Sur creates gnarly, mystical energy that flies out of your body, onto the pedals and into the wild blue yonder. You stop to gasp at the beauty at every ocean point vista overlook. Of all the wonder of the West Coast of America, the Big Sur captures your youth to leave memories for your lifetime.

Arduous climbs become triumphs for your spirit while the downhill roller coaster rides cause every cell in your body to cheer with joy. You yell out in sheer delight while you charge into another sunlit blue-sky curve delighting your world.

At one point on a vista outcrop point about 150 feet above a deep lagoon, we stopped for a drink. A lady sat on the rocks pointing out something to her husband who stood behind a 1,000 mm camera lens.

"There she blows," the lady said, pointing.

We looked down to see a 36-ton Gray whale surface and blow her 15-foot mist into the air. Around her, seawater cascaded down her sides to create bubbles in the water around her profile. The sun caught the bubbles to create a silver aura around her body. Seconds later, and her baby calf surfaced out of the greenish-blue lagoon and blew 15-foot high columns of mist into the morning air. The ocean water cascaded off the calf's body to create a foaming white "aura" silhouetting its gray frame. I grabbed my camera for a dozen shots of the miracle below me. They played in the lagoon for 10 minutes before heading north toward their Arctic feeding grounds in Alaska.

"Good grief," I muttered to Sandi. "Are we the luckiest cyclists on the coast this morning or what!"

At another point, a line of pelicans glided over the waves as they flew in formation just for me. Another 50 white seagulls flew one behind the other in a flying line of dental floss for my imagination. Behind them, a flock of 50 grey birds flew inches above the Pacific waters.

As we stood on the cliff, a 21-year-old girl and her friend hopped out of their red convertible Mustang.

"What are you two doing?" she said, pointing to my sign.

"We're riding from Canada to Mexico," I said.

"You're insane," she said, rather judgmentally. "Why don't you just drive a car?"

"Could you please make that, 'Insanely happy!'" I said.

"No, I'll keep with insane," she said.

"Have you seen that mother whale and her calf below us?" I said.

They stepped over to the side of the cliff to look. They spent all of a three-second glance.

"Whatever," one of the girls said. "Let's get out of here."

They jumped into their car and vanished around the next curve. I'm not certain, but the natural world may not be a priority to the younger generation.

Without a doubt the Big Sur creates "moments" that stay with you for your lifetime. Whether you write them down in your journal or they burn into your legs, you remember all of it.

At the next vista point, a small crowd watched five dolphins surfing the waves. We stopped to talk with them and share their wonder. It reminded us of a John Muir quote from years ago, "How many hearts with warm red blood in them are beating under the cover of woods and water, and how many teeth and eyes are shining? A multitude of animal people, intimately related to us, but of whose lives we know almost nothing, are as busy about their own affairs as we are about ours." January 1898

Chapter 1

OCEAN, SKY, FREEDOM—WEST COAST BICYCLE ADVENTURE—CANADA TO MEXICO

Chapter 1: Starting in Bellingham, Washington. Ride up to the Canadian border. Heading south into the old growth Douglas firs of the Washington rainforest.

"The mystique of bicycle travel fascinates modern Americans. Why would anyone "endure" the pains of providing their own locomotion via pedaling rather than the comfort and speed of a car, boat, plane or train? The answer lies in the antiquity of "pedaling bliss." It thrives in the meshing of your energy with the energy of the universe. It rushes into the secret corners of your mind to explore the world on your own terms. Too much comfort leads to tedium or the indolence of life. Once you swing your leg over the saddle of a bicycle, a whole new mental, physical and spiritual dimension opens to every cell in your body. You "fly" at the "perfect speed" with a comet's tail of memories following you into eternity." FHW

(Sandi and Frosty standing at the Canadian Border, north of
Bellingham, Washington for the beginning of the Canada
to Mexico, West Coast Bicycle Adventure.)

At the beginning of an adventure, your entire body elevates with excitement. Expectation races around your mind like a Coney Island rollercoaster. What might open for you on a pedal journey of thousands of miles? Who will you meet? What grand sights will you see? What will you learn from your travels?

Sandi and I landed in Bellingham, Washington in early July. We enjoyed sunny skies, warm weather and the promise of a great start for our Canada to Mexico West Coast Bicycle Adventure.

We assembled the bikes for the next two hours. With our panniers packed, our gear organized, our flags flying and our spirits high, we pedaled a few miles into Bellingham to eat at the Brandy Wine Kitchen. They created a killer-delicious Red Lentil soup. Along with salad and hot garlic bread out of the oven, we delighted ourselves with our culinary feast. Two glasses of red wine topped off our celebration of our adventure.

After eating, we pedaled north past beautiful waterfront homes with stylish porches and high-pitched roofs featuring elegant flower arrays surrounding yards and driveways.

Seagulls squawked across the airwaves of that coastal city. We rode through dense growth pines. We made it to the edge of town where we camped at a construction business in a nice patch of grass behind the main building that provided us privacy and quiet.

Bicycle touring allows "stealth camping" just about anywhere you ride in the world. We carry a tent, sleeping bags, air mattresses and a black cloth shower bag. It warms up the water on the back of the bike an hour before we camp. Nothing like a comforting shower at the end of a day of sweating.

Are there any rules to stealth camping? Yes! Find a spot behind a building, a stand of trees, over a hill out of sight of the road, beside a lake, stream or river. We've camped in cow pastures, sheep paddocks, junk yards, hay fields, behind stacked logs, in church yards, gas stations and schools. Sometimes, we ask folks if we can camp in their yards. We promise to leave their yard pristine.

At times, folks invite us in for dinner and they offer a spare bedroom. What do they ask in return? They want to hear about our best stories on the road. For certain, my wife Sandi tells a whale of a tale that excites all her listeners.

At the same time, for non-campers, you may use route maps by Adventure Cycling that will give you motels, campgrounds, Air B and B's, and WarmShowers hosts. The key: make your trip exactly as you like it with accommodations that fit your style.

In the morning, after a fabulous breakfast at the Hilltop Restaurant, we cranked up Route 539 for 25 miles to reach the Canadian Border. With a few shots from the tripod at the border fence, we headed south toward our destination of the Mexican border.

(Flowers at the Edelen Dairy Barn where they served
incredible ice cream straight from the creamery.)

At the border, we stopped at an ice cream-cheese-milk Edaleen Dairy
Barn that featured the best soft-serve we've ever tasted. They grew giant
baskets of flowers under some trees in their front yard. People from all over
the country stopped to buy their dairy products.

A Canadian Indian lady sat down beside us, "I hear you have bicycled
around the world."

"Who told you that?" I said.

"Your wife," she said.

"Well, yes ma'am, six continents with one more to go," I said. "What
kind of work do you do?"

"Well," she said. "I am a teacher at the reservation. Last week, I gave
the kids a writing assignment to go outside and write about what they saw."

"What did they write about?" I asked.

"They wrote about cars, houses, telephone lines, Facebook, Instagram,
etc." she said. "I was hoping they would write about blue skies, lady bugs
landing on their arms and the breeze blowing through the leaves. They

could have described a bird chirping, listening to the silence or watching a sunset. They could have portrayed an eagle nesting, going barefoot in the grass, or wading into a river, you know, stuff like that."

"Different set of parameters for kids today," I said. "They can't describe the natural world with their eyes chained to a smart phone. We keep moving further away from Nature toward the mechanical and computer world. Those kids are wired differently as they dial into their smart phones seven days a week. The farther we travel into the mechanical world, the more we lose our natural world vibrations and frequencies."

"You white people did that to us," she said. "We used to live in the old ways until you pulled the rug out from under us. Now we have spiritual poverty and emotionally starving children."

"Can't argue with you on that one," I said.

"Truth is truth," she said, without malice.

"Blessings to you," Sandi said.

She stood up, threw her napkin into the trash can, walked over to her car, and drove off.

Having read much of what happened to the aborigines of North America, I felt her anguish. We used mechanized violence to subdue them while we stuck them onto "reservations" or what might be called "internment camps." We supplied them with booze, disease and welfare. We deleted their way of life, their freedoms, their religions, their languages and their land. She wasn't too happy with us.

While on the road, everyone tells you his or her story. One other guy came over to talk about his retirement. He told us his life story with divorces, kids, bosses, hating his job, drinking and finally, living alone after his wife died of cancer. He decided to travel the world each summer with his remaining years.

"I made a lot of mistakes in my life," he said. "But the good Lord willing, I'm working to share kindness with everyone from here on out."

From the border, we pedaled back down Route 539 also named "Mount Baker Highway." A huge snow-covered peak shined off to the east of us. It struck majestically into the sky. We stopped at several lakes with hundreds of ducks floating in the still waters.

We pedaled back into Bellingham where we ate dinner at the same restaurant from the night before.

"If you guys are looking for a camping spot," a patron said. "You can go eight miles on Route 11 to Larrabee State Park in the deep woods. From there you can connect with Route 20 and Whidbey Island all the way to the ferry that takes you to Port Townshend."

"Thank you," said Sandi.

(My bike Condor and a bed of flowers growing inside a manure spreader.)

We pedaled out of town with the sun shining over the bay with big cargo ships anchored in the water. The road led to Chuckanut Drive along the inlet through deep woods. The rainforest covered the road like a green tunnel. Sandi passed in and out of the fading light. It created a magical glow replete with greens, leaves and waving grass.

We traveled through a silent green forest tunnel. We pedaled through the afternoon into the "sweet spot" of cycling where the air temperature dropped from hot to cool, where it perfected itself on our senses. Cycling into such an ethereal zone enhanced our spirits with a new and delightful tranquility in the moment.

Up and down we traveled through nature's light show. Finally, we arrived at the park where we pitched our tent on top of a mound of grass with massive spruce, ferns and Douglas firs: untouched.

"This is magical," said Sandi.

"Paradise," I said.

(Sandi pedaling through the "sweet spot" of perfection as the sun dropped through the trees and the temperature cooled us on the final leg of the day to Larrabee State Park.)

Chapter 2

PORT TOWNSEND AND SAILING SHIPS

Chapter 2: Sleeping vibrations in boreal forests, Edward R. Murrow journalist, homemade soups and pies, Deception Bay.

"When you sleep under 1,000-year-old trees, they impart their vibrations into your body. They stand guard over your emotions, dreams and aspirations. It's almost like the negative vibrations of living drain into the ground and the positive vibrations of the planet upload into your cells. During the stillness of the night, the stars filter through the deep green needles while water from a nearby brook gurgles with a rhythmic trance that lulls your mind into quiet solitude. A quiet sleep in the deep forest beats any night at a Holiday Inn." FHW

(Sandi on the road to Anacortes, Washington, southbound on the famous
Route 101 along the West Coast also known as the Pacific Coast Highway.)

"Honey," said Sandi in the morning. "I'm hungry. Let's find a
restaurant."

We packed our gear within 45 minutes, cleaned the campsite and hit
the pedals. We traveled south along Route 11 through morning moisture
and sunshine piercing the leaf cover.

A few miles later saw us riding along the ocean with oyster beds and
shellfish farms neatly cultivating the ocean's endless food chain.

Finally, we stopped for breakfast at "The Edison Café 1939", Edison,
Washington 98232 on Facebook. Linda and Lisa, two attractive blonds
served-up delicious oatmeal with all the trimmings. For dessert, Linda
baked a killer raspberry pie. She also served up mouthwatering tomato
basil soup for the soon-to-be lunch crowd.

(Stopping to eat at the famous Edison Cafe where the famous
journalist Edward R. Murrow started his life.)

As we relaxed in that old Texaco gas station, I noted pictures of
Edward R. Murrow, the famous journalist and TV reporter who told it like
it "was" instead of what transpires with the spin for whomever shows the
most money in 21st century America. He grew up in Edison, played high
school basketball and launched his career as a world traveler and reporter.
It shows that humble beginnings cannot stop anyone with a vision for his
or her life, and endless energy to pursue it.

"You ready to ride Sandi?" I asked.

"How about one more piece of raspberry pie?" she said.

"Have at it, girl," I said.

Sandi loves to eat. This bike ride guarantees her hunger levels to jump
off the chart. That's okay, because she can eat all she wants since bicycling
accelerates calorie burning.

We talked to several other touring cyclists on the same route, but they
pedaled much faster than us. We marveled at the beauty of the countryside
and small towns right out of the 1930's. Rural America remains a fabulous
place to live.

We pedaled through farm fields growing potatoes, corn and wheat. We cranked along flat land with trees lining the road.

Black birds, robins, crows and sparrows flitted through the air in great numbers. We kept pedaling until Route 20 cut left at the Fidalgo Country Inn. We stopped for the night. We enjoyed comforting hot showers and food from the restaurant.

Up at sunrise, we hit the road to ride through deep forest green woods and glimpses of the inlets along the route. Vast tidal plains lay exposed with low tide. We pedaled through Anacortes and ever-deepening rainforest woods until Puget Sound opened up to a blue expanse with fog banks rolling across the waters.

We swept around several lakes until we arrived at Deception Bay.

(Sandi in front of Deception Bay Bridge with the fog
rolling over the top in the background.)

Riding through dense rainforest, we arrived along an inlet from the Pacific Ocean. Ahead of us, a wild, swirling mist swept over Deception Bay Bridge.

"Wow! Look at that mist curling over the top of the bridge," I said to Sandi.

"It looks magical coming off the ocean," she said.

A sign read: The swirling waters that pass between the narrow inlet between Whidbey Island and Fidalgo Island have captivated visitors to this area for thousands of years. Native American tribes were the first to inhabit these islands and navigated these waters in cedar canoes as they traveled westward to the San Juan's to fish. The first explorers to chart these islands in the 1700's mistakenly assumed the two islands to be part of the mainland and thought the powerful currents came from a mighty river to the east. Captain George Vancouver realized the mistake and named it "Deception Pass" in 1792 when he explored the Northwest Passage.

(Sandi looking out to the fog rolling in over the
Pacific Ocean toward Deception Bay.)

We snapped several shots standing on rock fences as the mist swept up the channel and over the bridge. From there, we walked our bikes over the bridge on a narrow sidewalk meant for only one person. We pulled our traffic-side safety flags off the bikes to let other walkers past us.

Sandi looked out toward the blue Pacific.

"This fog is SO beautiful," she said. "Look at the islands out there and fishing boats, plus all those diving birds. This is a birdwatcher's paradise."

"Sure is," I said. "Gees, it must be 200 feet from the bridge to the water."

"Yeah, here comes a barge carrying a crane," said Sandi.

We snapped several pictures before continuing toward Oak Harbor, Washington. We loaded up on food before heading to the ferry, which would carry us to Port Townsend.

We pedaled through more forests and farmland until we reached a savannah and the ferry. We made it with only two minutes to spare. We rolled the bikes onto the car deck, secured them to the bike racks and walked upstairs to the main passenger deck. Blue water and beautiful mountains greeted us to the west. About 45 minutes later, we steamed into Port Townsend, Washington, the "Seafaring Port of the Northwest" from back in the 1800's when visionaries built the town as the trading post of Pacific Northwest.

(Sandi pedaling off the ferry in Port Townsend, Washington.)

Downtown Port Townsend featured elegant brick hotels, restaurants and businesses right out of the old west. We saw 1887 marked on the fronts of most of the buildings.

At dinner, we sat in a fancy hotel looking out the windows at the streets realizing that generations of visitors dined and stared out the same windows over 140 years ago. They endured dirt streets and horse-drawn carriages while we enjoyed pavement and cars.

As twilight fell, we pedaled to the edge of town where we found a cement pavilion behind an abandoned restaurant. We pitched the tent behind the building, plugged our computer into a socket and quickly fell asleep.

(Typical hotel from 1886 in downtown Port Townsend, Washington.)

Chapter 3

OCEAN, SKY, FREEDOM—STEALTH CAMPING

Chapter 3: Making your life-mate happy! Coffee delirium with 'Better Living Through Coffee', into the Olympic rainforest, 50's diner and iron statues.

"Sometimes, while bicycle touring, you never know where you might pitch your tent for a night's sleep. Stealth camping allows you dramatic opportunities. Near twilight, you watch for a quiet country road that vanishes into the trees. You search for an abandoned building at the side of a town to camp behind. You try to spy a river or lake for the perfect campfire. No matter what, when people ask you where you're staying for the night, you say, 'Somehow, every night, the 'perfect camp spot' makes itself known to me.' In over four decades of bicycle adventures, Mother Nature provides elegant camping sites." FHW

What makes you happy when you wake up in the morning? Sandi loves a steaming cup of gourmet coffee. It's her daily ritual.

At dawn, we awoke from a long night's sleep.

"Let's go back to that coffee shop on Main Street," said Sandi. "I think it was named 'Better Living Through Coffee.'"

"Works for me," I said.

We packed out bikes. A quick ride down a quiet Main Street brought us to a funky coffee shop. Many people stood in line for coffee and pastries. We sat by the window on the water to watch some ducks swimming around. Later, a deer with two babies walked right along the water's edge. Out in the bay, the aircraft carrier Nimitz released from its docking and steamed out of the harbor. Truly a massive floating piece of iron with an airstrip!

"That's a monster ship," I said.

"This is the best coffee I have ever savored," said Sandi. "I adore its exquisite taste. Oh, yes, that's a big ship."

I read the menu, "'We serve traditionally prepared, nutrient-dense food and baked items all made on site. Our food menu is based on the wisdom of Nourishing Traditions and the work of Sally Fallon and Weston Price. We also offer vegan and gluten free foods for those with dietary restrictions.'"

"I am so happy," said Sandi. "This is the best coffee of my life. Divine!"

(County building in Port Townsend. Beautiful architecture.)

We couldn't help but notice the magnificent buildings created by the contractors back in the 1880's. The huge hotels with exquisite facades exhibited a much more ornate era with simpler realities in America and the world.

Each building featured tall windows with ornate cherry wood and tall wooden doors. Lavish facades decorated the buildings to present an artistic flair unknown today.

One could imagine the sailors and Dapper Dan's with uptown ladies on their arms sashaying along the bustling streets. By the 1890's, the railroads couldn't make it through the swamps to create a main line into North America. The town dried up. Big money men lost millions on their speculation.

We found it difficult to pedal out of that beautiful, historic town. It felt stuck in its own past and time zone. It's almost as if America's civilization would have been better off if we stopped "progress" right at that time. Much more uncomplicated: simpler, easier, basic, slower, quieter and calmer.

Later, we pedaled through the deep woods out of Port Townsend on Route 101. We rolled along Hood Canal. Green trees lined the road, along with an up and down highway with serpentine curves. It carried us southward.

(1930's dump truck and many other old farmers' tractors
dotted the landscape as we rolled south.)

In the morning, we cruised through cool mist. As we traveled along the canal, fishing boats, sailboats and cabins dotted the landscape. After a long day in the saddle, we could not find a camping spot to save our lives. Finally, as night fell, we spotted a grassy spot near the water.

Next morning, we watched birds skimming over the surface of the canal as the sun rose into the sky.

We pedaled along the canal where vendors sold king salmon and other seafoods. Many businesses depended on the salmon runs. We saw countless fishermen, luxury fishing boats and sailboats. Around noon, we reached Shelton where we ate at the Three Sisters Restaurant. After stuffing ourselves, we snapped a few shots of Sandi beside an 1800's steam locomotive.

We rolled out of Shelton straight south toward Raymond. Logging country! Big trucks blasted by us. Then, rain spit into our faces. The air turned cool. We sweated, then chilled, and then sweated on the undulating highway.

"Now I know why it's so green," said Sandi. "So much rain!"

We pedaled through ugly 'clear cuts' where the lumbermen cut down everything in sight for miles. They stripped the land down to tree stumps and rock. It's quite unpleasant to see up close. On an ecological level, it meant that all the animals lost their homes, which forced them to invade other homes of other established creatures in the remaining forests. Unfortunately, the human race doesn't know when to quit. It expands, encroaches and destroys wildlife habitat. That means 250 creatures suffer extinction every year in the United States as our population continues to grow by 3.1 million, net gain, annually. Sad to say that no one speaks for the wildlife and their rights to their homes.

After pedaling for 35 miles, we reached Raymond at sunset. We found a beautiful motel inside the small town. We showered up, dressed up and walked to a 1950's "Slater's Diner" where burgers, fries and shakes took us back into the same era as the movie "Grease." Lots of 1957 Chevys, Corvettes, Elvis and Doris Day!

An additional treat greets visitors to Raymond: intriguing iron statues commemorating the loggers, trains and farmers who worked the land.

(Texaco at 29.9 cents per gallon. Now those were the good old days!)

Chapter 4

ELVIS AND MARILYN MONROE

Chapter 4: Elvis Presley, Marilyn Monroe, old-fashioned strawberry milk shake in steel can, 57' Chevy muscle cars, Juke Box and "Pretty Woman."

"Bicycling unites physical harmony coupled with emotional bliss to create a sense of spiritual perfection that combines your body, mind and soul into a single moving entity. You, the cyclist, power your steel steed with two spoked metal rims wrapped in rubber tires toward the distant horizon. That far off place where the sky meets the earth, holds promise on multiple levels. Bicycling allows a person to mesh with the sun, sky and road as if nothing else mattered in the world. At the perfect speed, you flow unerringly toward your destiny. In fact, all your worries, cares and troubles vanish in the rear-view mirror while you bicycle along the highways of the world: you pedal as one with the universe." FHW

(Everybody loves traveling whether by sailboat,
canoe, raft, steamer, plane, jet or bicycle.)

Next morning, we awoke to pouring rain. Big lumber trucks hauled huge logs into the mill for cutting. We smelled the heavy scent of freshly cut trees.

"I'm not excited to pedal in this all-day downpour," said Sandi.

"Okay, let's stay another night in the motel," I said. "I think they have a hot tub."

"Hot tub, yes!" she said with a smile.

We lounged, watched TV and read most of the day. As the evening settled around us, the rain abated.

"Let's eat at the diner," Sandi said. "I loved their soup, salad, eggplant and milk shakes."

We walked out into the misty ocean light; just the right touch of freshly scrubbed air, glistening green forests and sunset through the clouds. We walked five blocks to the diner. Along the way, we saw a dozen flat, metal sculptures dotting the city streets. Each depicted farming, logging and pioneer life.

Along the streets, 100-year-old homes housed a lot of families, kids and middle-class life from hardworking Americans. In some of the side yards, old 57' Chevys, 66' Ford Thunderbirds and a few Plymouths caught my attention. Since I come from that era, those old cars made me feel like a kid again. I drove a 1953 and 1957 Chevy two-door.

(Who doesn't love the myth and magic of Marilyn Monroe and Elvis Presley?)

At the diner, we admired Elvis Presley and Marilyn Monroe posters decorating the walls. Lots of 50's and 60's "Muscle Cars" gave the place a feel for our baby boomer past. They featured an old Juke Box into which we shoved a few quarters to listen to Ray Orbison with his "Pretty woman, walking down the street…." along with Elvis' "Jailhouse Rock" and "Can't help falling in love with you."

Funny thing about living our youth in the 50's and 60's with special times like "Happy Days" and a huge transition from the old ways of agrarian living to our high speed, technological society of today. From the pace of horses to the speed of intercontinental jets. We changed from cooking our own food to microwaved instant dinners.

Often, given all the craziness happening to America, I wish we could have stabilized our civilization around those simpler, saner and safer "good old days."

In the morning, the sun sparkled in the sky. We devoured a special oatmeal breakfast with toast and homemade jam. Gotta' love it!

We pedaled through more clear cuts, back into thick green forests and closer to the Oregon state line.

The journey through southwest Washington State crosses through ancient Native American lands. They lived and fished the abundant waters of the Columbia River.

In the late afternoon, we cut south on Route 401 to reach the legendary Columbia River.

European explorers like Captain Robert Gray charted the location of the river mouth in 1792. Lewis and Clark with 33 mountain men, ended their quest to find the Northwest Passage at the mouth of the Columbia River in 1804-1805. We passed "Dismal Nitch" where they camped for several days to withstand a nasty Pacific Ocean storm that nearly blew them back up the river. Once the storm abated, they paddled across the four-mile-wide expanse of the river to the current town of Astoria. The town's name stems from the fur baron, John Jacob Astor, who bought all the furs and sold them to the top hat and fashion shops of New York City. "Fashion" nearly caused the extinction of beavers, foxes, minks, and other furry creatures. From where the "Corps of Discovery" landed on the south side of the river, they searched for a place to build a fort for winter quarters.

"It's so meaningful to see actual history right in front of our eyes," Sandi said. "I mean, we're standing right where Lewis and Clark camped out. I bet it would have been pretty dismal to sit in wet tents, wet gear and cold rains for a week. They must have been tough mountain men to survive such terrible odds."

"You wouldn't be wrong," I said. "How they survived 4,100 miles from St. Louis, Missouri on boats, canoes, walking, horseback, in addition to mountain passes, snows, rains, sleet, starvation and grizzly bears…well, those boys proved themselves tougher than nails."

We pedaled toward the Megler Bridge profiled on the far side of the point in front of us. We passed old, broken sailing ships and abandoned barges.

We passed by abandoned wharfs inhabited by seagulls and cormorants sunning themselves on protruding logs from the decaying docks.

(Raymond, Washington features dozens of metal statues
depicting some form of pioneer, logging and farm life.)

With a hard left, we began our odyssey over the 4.1-mile long Megler Bridge. Hundreds of seagulls guided us as they soared on the updrafts created by the bridge ramparts. After 30 minutes, we reached the last mile where the bridge climbed sharply about 300 feet above the water. To our left, three ocean-going freighters anchored in the deep waters. To our right, the endless Pacific Ocean stretched all the way to the horizon.

(Sandi after riding over the Megler Bridge which spans the Columbia River
where Lewis and Clark first arrived upon the Pacific Ocean back in 1805.)

At the end of the day, our bodies meshed with the rhythm of the road. We hit that sweet spot where our cells co-mingled with the energy of the highway. Our minds flowed with the breeze passing by our faces. Our pedals floated above the ground in their own flight of fancy. Some call it an "endorphin high." It happens at the most surprising of times. Our bodies glided gleefully down the road. A certain magic transformed our journey into physical, mental and spiritual Zen.

After completing Washington State, we celebrated by stopping at the "Pig and Pancake Restaurant" for dinner. Our server, a lady named Olive asked us to write her a note once we reached Mexico. She said, "I will never get to live such an incredible adventure…it would be nice to know that you finished the ride."

"We'll do that," I said.

In fact, I sent her a copy of this book to let her know that she too, rode with us. When she received a copy, her smile lit up the room.

After stuffing ourselves, we clicked on our red blinking taillights to follow Route 101 south. Quickly, we found a smooth green lawn behind a "For Sale" automobile repair shop.

Sleep came easily and peacefully.

"If, in after years, I should do better in the way of exact research, then these lawless wanderings will not be without value as suggestive beginnings. But if I should be fated to walk no more with Nature, be compelled to leave all I most devoutly love in the wilderness, return to civilization and be twisted into the characterless cable of society, then these sweet, freed, cumberless rovings will be as chinks and slits on life's horizon, through which I may obtain glimpses of the treasures that lie in God's wilds beyond my reach." John Muir, wilderness man, 1872

Chapter 5

LEWIS & CLARK TRAIL

Chapter 5: Lewis & Clark Corps of Discovery, Oregon coast, Fort Clatsop, Haystack Rock

"Have you ever wondered what causes all this beauty we cycle through? What created the energy of trees, rocks and that eternal ocean off to our right as we pedal south? What makes that sky above us change so often in only an hour? What creates the magnificent rivers we cross on our two-wheeled journey? Do you contemplate deeply while pedaling your bicycle? Do you feel the essence of the creative energy of the universe pulsing through everything around you? It streams through rocks, plants, birds, wind, fire, water and animals. It vibrates through you. Some call it God or the Great Spirit or other countless names. Whatever your own choice, its presence in the universe created this incredible planet on which we play during our lives. For that, I am thankful for my brief moment of existence. On my bicycle, I recognize an enormous amount of energy coursing through all the cells in my body because I travel down the road with a happy heart and a big smile on my face. Bet you do, too!" FHW

We entered Astoria, Oregon named for the famous fur trader John Jacob Astor. He bought all the furs from trappers to feed the fashion industry in New York and Paris. Astoria became the shipping hub of the Northwest. Ships from all over the world sailed into the dangerous waters of the Columbia River. Because of shoals and sandbars, over 700 ships met their watery grave in the past 200 years. It's also known as the "Graveyard of the Pacific."

We visited the "Maritime Museum" in the middle of town on the waterfront. The museum offered a tremendous and interesting history of the area. Big cruise liners docked for a day or two. They added 4,000 people to the town for 24 hours, and then, steamed off toward Alaska or other ports unknown.

That night, we camped at Fort Stevens State Park. In the morning, we stopped at Fort Clatsop, sight of the 1804-1806 winter quarters of Lewis & Clark's Corps of Discovery Expedition. In November 1805 after reaching the Pacific Ocean, the men built the fort in two weeks from the surrounding forest. They chose an ample water source and plenty of wild game for food. They named the fort after the Clatsop Indians who lived in the area. During their four months at the fort, they enjoyed only six sunny days and six cloudy days. It rained the rest of the time. They endured freezing cold temperatures, mice, rashes, bedbugs and close quarters. Daily rains kept them pretty miserable. In the spring of 1806, they paddled their canoes back up the Columbia River, rode horses across the mountains, canoed down the Yellowstone and Missouri Rivers, and back to St. Louis, Missouri. They retraced their entire journey to make it back on September 23, 1806.

During their epic trek, they survived grizzly bears, hostile Native Americans, starvation, mosquitoes, incredible obstacles, disease and the unknown. A famous Indian maiden, Sacagawea, saved them from certain death at one point during the journey.

After the Corps returned, Meriwether Lewis found himself in trouble with alcohol, rejection from females, financial debt, and is thought to have been killed by robbers or committed suicide. Sgt. Ordway wrote an excellent journal about the entire journey. Most Americans cannot conceive the enormity of the expanse and breadth of the trip. They paddled oar boats, walked, rode horseback and canoed over 4,100 miles at a pace of five miles per hour or less. If you ever visit Great Falls, Montana, please check out the "Lewis & Clark Interpretative Center" for a firsthand experience of their extraordinary adventure.

After spending the morning at Fort Clatsop, we curled along Route 101 through Gearheart, Seaside and on to Canon Beach. Dramatic views of the Pacific Ocean mesmerized us.

At Canon Beach, we walked around that captivating town of art shops, kite shops, deli's, chocolate shops and restaurants. We frolicked on the beach. We enjoyed a lazy day filled with fun people on their own adventures.

Near sundown, we pedaled out of town until we reached Haystack Rock, which rose dramatically out of the ocean to a height of 254 feet within 100 yards of the beach. Birds flew all around it as the sun boiled into the ocean. Hundreds of Tufted Puffins flew everywhere. Seagulls, ducks, pelicans and other sea birds skimmed the waves, flew in groups, fluttered wildly and caused the air to become a wild display of airborne magic.

We discovered a campground in the forest on the edge of town to bed down for the night. Nothing like a hot shower, clean clothes and a warm sleeping bag to complete the day!

In the morning, we awoke to squawking seagulls and crashing beach waves.

The road led us through Arch Cape, Manzanita and Wheeler on Route 101. In the last town, we rode up on fifteen 1929 Ford cars painted in various colors.

(Sandi in front of the 1920's Ford cars.)

"This looks like a collection right out of the 1920's," said Sandi. "I feel like Henry Ford might walk out of the restaurant to greet us."

"Let's go talk to all the folks who drive these cars," I said. "Plus, I'm hungry for a big bowl of oatmeal loaded with blueberries."

Inside, we introduced ourselves to the folks driving the antique Fords. They dressed the part in their costumes. We enjoyed a great deal of banter about bicycles and horseless carriages.

"Just remember this," one fellow said. "Henry Ford said, 'If you think you can, or you think you can't; you're right.'"

Sandi said, "I've always figured I can, and I have!"

"Life is good," the older man said.

We continued our trek south until we reached the town of Garibaldi where we ate dinner. Later, we found a quiet campsite deep within a blackberry patch. Nothing like stuffing our faces full of delicious, ripe blackberries surrounding us.

The one thing we enjoy as senior citizens stems from the fact that a blackberry patch returns us to our childhoods. With one bite of a juicy plump blackberry, it carries us back to the kitchen with mom canning corn, peas, tomatoes, applesauce and blackberry jam. Do you remember the Mason or Ball jars? That taste of your youth lingers on the tip of your tongue. While it's not a daily party being post 70 years old, we sure enjoy our "youthful" experiences on our bicycles.

In the morning, we returned to another restaurant in town. A museum showed us pictures of what the town looked like at the turn of the century. A huge hotel and docking area located near the water once helped manage logs waiting to be processed. The only thing left from that era: a huge 200-foot high chimney stood over the town.

(Countless historical signs along the highway educated
us as to the events of the West Coast.)

In the Garibaldi Maritime Museum, we discovered Captain Gray, the first American to sail around the world. He navigated his ship, the Columbia, a short distance up the river, which ultimately became its name.

After an educational visit to the museum, we pedaled our way 12 miles to the Tillamook Cheese Factory. We savored some of the most delicious ice cream on the planet. The factory showed the early beginnings of cheese-making in the area. Today, it's world famous.

(Sandi stretching her wings by the Tillamook Cheese Factory.)

After our fill of cheese-covered French-fries and ice cream, we headed out on Route 131 to Cape Meares Lighthouse. Later, we camped in a clear-cut part of the forest near the lighthouse as night fell quickly. We pitched our tent in the old growth forest with mist wafting through the Douglas Firs. Climbing into our sleeping bags, the quiet of the wilderness lulled us to sleep.

We awoke to fog, trees and sublime silence. The road led to the coast and breakfast at a seaside restaurant. We gobbled tasty pancakes with maple syrup and scrambled eggs.

After stuffing ourselves, we pedaled along an estuary where dozens of Chinese, Vietnamese and other groups dug for shellfish, oysters and crabs in the low tide pools.

Soon, we climbed for three miles to Cape Lookout for fabulous views of the Pacific Ocean. We rode through dense old growth forests with sunshine spraying through the leaves for dramatic light columns playing on the forest floor.

Soon, we reached Cape Lookout (which means 'jut of land') with a large bar and restaurant. One hundred cars parked on the beach, but few people ventured into the surf because of the freezing cold North Pacific water. Most enjoyed the beach with sweatshirts, hoodies and nylon jacks.

Later in the day, we reached Neskowin (place of many fish) to bed down in the local motel. We ate a fabulous dinner at the "Creek Café" along a small river flowing out of the mountains to the ocean. Dessert? Yes! Cheesecake with strawberry sauce dripping down the sides! As the old man said, "Life is good!"

John Muir said, "The air is distinctly fragrant with balsam, resin and mint, every breath of it a gift we may well thank the Creator. Who could ever guess that so rough a wilderness should yet be so fine, so full of good things? One seems to be in a majestic domed pavilion in which a grand play is being acted with scenery, music and incense. All the furniture and action are so interesting we are in no danger of being called on to endure one dull moment. God himself seems to be always doing his best here, working like a man in a glow of enthusiasm." 1875

Chapter 6

WHALES AND DEPOE BAY

Chapter 6: Conde McCollough bridge of art, mermaids, sailing ships and the Sea Hag

"The long-distance touring cyclists pedal all over the planet without causing any environmental stress to Mother Nature. Therefore, the cyclist becomes an intricate part of the natural world. Not only that, he or she shares a magical connection that transcends the mechanized world. Every cell in a cyclist's body charges around thinking that it conquered the world. You might call it the "Eat, Pedal, Sleep" of life or for lack of another word, the transcendent joy of being alive." FHW

After eating a delicious waffle and oatmeal breakfast at the Hawk Creek Café, we lazed around the picnic tables on thick green grass to talk with other travelers. One older couple approached us, "We wish we were younger so we could do what you two are doing."

"Gosh, you don't look very old," Sandi said.

"Gordon just hit 66 last month," the wife said.

"Guess what," said Sandi. "We're older than you! I'm 70 and my husband is 73."

"Gasp!"

"No, you can't be," the husband said.

"Yes, we're both senior citizens and older than you," said Sandi.

"What's your secret?" asked the lady.

I answered, "Drugs, sex and rock n roll!"

They about fell over from laughing so hard.

Which brings me to a question: How old is too old to ride a bicycle on tour for a few days, week or month, and even longer? If you've read any of my other adventure books (please visit my website provided at the end of this book and click the "book" tab), you were introduced to older women bicycling around the world. While I paddled a canoe down Old Man River, I met two brothers, 76 and 78, canoeing the length of the Mississippi River at 2552 miles from Lake Itasca, Minnesota to New Orleans.

One old man I met, Verlen Kruger, canoed from the Arctic Ocean to the bottom of South America using the river systems. One 74-year old lady I met rode across America in a cart pulled by a donkey. One fellow I met on the road kicked a soccer ball coast to coast across America. Another ran the entire length of Route 66 from Chicago to Santa Monica Pier, California. His name is Dave Carder and we remain very good friends.

Two old ladies Sandi and I met on the Lewis & Clark Trail along the Columbia River Gorge announced to us their "gay" lifestyle and bragged that they were the first married couple of their sexual orientation to ride bicycles across America.

What I discovered: everybody at every age carries a secret passion. Many don't act on it. Many make excuses. The ones that do take action, however, well, you see them in far flung adventures around the planet. At any given moment, 60-70-80-year-olds bicycle, canoe, sail, raft, train, windsurf and fly around the world to fulfill their bucket lists before St. Peter invites them through the Pearly Gates.

After two hours of talking to various folks from all over the country, we decided to pedal south. We enjoyed a lovely stay in Neskowin with its abundant flowers, shops, delicious food and warm showers at the motel.

(Sandi posing by flower boxes in a yard in Neskowin.)

After leaving Neskowin, we rolled over countless 500-foot elevation mountain passes, which yielded tremendous views of the deep green Oregon wilderness.

What makes Oregon so green? Answer: rain! It started slowly with sprinkles, then a steady drizzle until the heavens opened up with their version of Hurricane Katrina.

We pulled-on our rain gear to stay dry, but we perspired from the heat of pedaling so we still felt wetness. We rode through rain and fog. Our flags flapped and our red blinking lights let rear traffic know our location on the highway. We turned on our white LED blinking lights for oncoming traffic to keep them alert to our presence. We wore yellow rain jackets to make sure drivers saw us.

Pedaling through the rain resembles slogging through the woods, walking through wet cement, sweating while you get drenched, enduring rain splashes in your face while you feel trapped in a moving shower stall. We endured and persevered.

One writer said, "Adventure is 10 percent discovery and 90 percent drudgery."

That comment raises a question about the efficacy of bicycle adventure travel. What about when you must pedal across the Great Plains of America for 1,000 miles? Or, how about pedaling over 1,200 miles down the Atacama Desert in South America? Nothing but sand and scorching temperatures! What about crossing nearly 2,000 miles of the Nullarbor Plains across Australia in 115-degree daily heat? How about pedaling through endless miles of the Amazon rainforest? Rain day after day! How about cranking up steep 8,000 to 12,000-foot passes along the "Spine of Rockies" on the Continental Divide in America?

Since I've ridden those rides, yes, I verify that thousands of those miles around this planet mean enduring the ravages of repetition, nothingness and oblivion. I can't say it's a party on two wheels. I can't say it's enthralling or exciting. At the same time, whether you climb mountains or scuba dive beneath the waves or paraglide through emptiness of the biosphere—something pulls the human spirit onward.

It sure pulls me! In the process of that 'pull' or 'tug' on my spirit, I've lived a thousand lives more than if I had sat in a rocking chair with all the comforts of home.

Creative living via bicycle travel offers you a different set of parameters. Bicycle touring enhances those opportunities beyond average living. Sure, during a rainstorm, you endure. Crossing a hot desert, you soak your clothes in sweat. Without a doubt, riding in the mountains lets you know you're alive. That next mountain pass costs you some calories and muscle burn. Especially at our plus 70 ages, it's toilsome. And yet, it's wonderful to triumph through the challenges.

Vigorous physical activity lets a human being know he or she lives—not merely exists.

"Pedaling Bliss" captivates every cell in my body. I press down on the power stroke that frees me from the world's troubles, anguish and pain. I notice that my legs become my wings and that, I am forever flying just off the pavement to wherever the road takes me.

I love knowing I am alive. I love knowing I can transport myself over extreme distances. I love the emotional, mental and physical engagement of my senses. Do you love something that "turns you on" in every cell of your body? Good! You know what I mean. It's the Zen experience of your life. I don't give a darn about the rain! I pedal through it until I see a rainbow.

Sandi and I recommend that if you want to take such an adventuresome bicycle ride, try out a touring company for a three-day weekend, or a week, or more. You can enjoy first class tours with motels and all meals served. Adventure Cycling Magazine offers every type of bicycle tour to fit your needs. You can take barge trips on the rivers in Europe where you eat breakfast on the barge, bicycle all day to special places, and return to dine in luxury on the Rhein River, and then, sleep all night as the barge takes you to the next destination. Talk about tons of fun! If you face physical challenges, they offer E-bikes that assist your pedaling efforts. They also offer hand-crank bikes for those who love to pedal but have lost the use of their legs. Those bikes put the "fun" of cycling back into your world.

On down the road, we reached a spit of land on Boiler Bay. As the wind blew vigorously, the waves raced into the rocks to crash into outrageous white mountains of spray. It's constant, raging fury pounding against the black rocks. Boiler Bay might be one of the wildest pictures of Nature's energy on the whole West Coast ride.

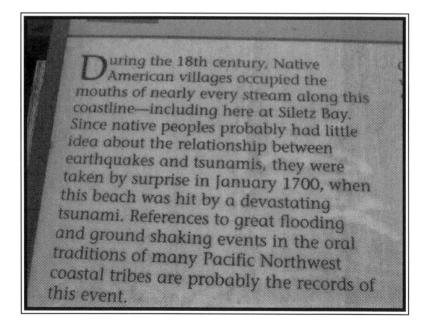

During the 18th century, Native American villages occupied the mouths of nearly every stream along this coastline—including here at Siletz Bay. Since native peoples probably had little idea about the relationship between earthquakes and tsunamis, they were taken by surprise in January 1700, when this beach was hit by a devastating tsunami. References to great flooding and ground shaking events in the oral traditions of many Pacific Northwest coastal tribes are probably the records of this event.

(Travel allows everyone to enjoy the history of areas they visit.)

Later, we passed Fogarty Creek into Depoe Bay. What a beautiful town right out of the 1800's! City planners built walkways around the bay to see the seabirds, whales and seals! Big gray whales swam right into the deep waters of the bay. When they exhaled through their blowholes, a fountain of spray shot 15-feet into the air.

"Look at that one," said Sandi as she stood inside the National Park Service "Whale Watch" station on the edge of a cliff in Depoe Bay.

"Wow," I said. "This is an outdoor zoo with no bars or cages."

A big gray whale broke the water for her breath of air and instantly vanished below the waves. The ranger reported 87 sightings that day. Some of them stay all summer because the food-chain keeps them thriving.

Gray whales run 36 tons, 40 feet long and live up to 70 years. They migrate from the Mexican Baja where they birth their young to the Alaskan waters where they fatten up on the rich food sources. Around 26,000 of them remain since we stopped allowing unlimited harpooning of those docile creatures. They can be seen during their annual migrations all along the coast of Washington, Oregon and California.

(Seals resting on the rocks in Depoe Bay.)

Later, we ate lunch at the Sea Hag. What's so cool about dining at that ancient establishment? Sailors from 120 years ago ate breakfast, lunch and dinners at the Sea Hag. You can smell the past in the hardwood floors, doors and booths.

Back on the road, fog prevailed. Nonetheless, a short distance out of town on Otter Creek, we saw a colony of seals sleeping on the rocks. The whole area sports 200-foot cliffs, rugged rocks, ocean waves crashing everywhere and seabirds floating or flying. Later, we stopped by the Devil's Punch Bowl where the ocean pounded up into the lava rock, creating wild spray plumes.

Along the Pacific Coast Highway Route 101, we passed lighthouses from the 1800's that kept frigate ships from smashing onto the rocks. We pedaled past stunning beach formations with eternal waves crashing and smashing again and again onto the lava rocks in this region known as the "Ring of Fire" where Mt. St. Helens blew up in 1980.

After a long day, we decided to hang it up in Newport, Oregon near one of the historic Conde McCollough bridges. He designed and built them in the 1920's. Riding over them feels like pedaling through art and history at the same time.

Admittedly, this day tested us. At the same time, I thought about that old guy telling me that adventure equates to 90 percent drudgery. If I look back at the pictures and moments of this day, you know something, I'll take the entire package of adventure any day. As John Muir said, "We're watching the handwriting of God."

Chapter 7

DEVIL'S CHURN, BRIDGE OF ART

Chapter 7: Dining room with a view of Conde McCollough Bridge, Devil's Churn, Cape Perpetua.

"When I go biking, I repeat a mantra of the day's sensations: bright sun, blue sky, warm breeze, blue jay's call, ice melting and so on. This helps me transcend the traffic, ignore the clamorings of work, leave all the mind theaters behind and focus on Nature instead. I still must abide by the rules of the road, of biking, of gravity. But I am mentally far away from civilization. The world is breaking someone else's heart."
~Diane Ackerman

(Sandi riding across the magical, artistic and stupendous
Conde McCollough Yaquina Bridge out of Newport.)

After reaching Newport, Oregon, we settled into a quiet motel room on the beach. One of the locals suggested a fabulous dinner at a restaurant in Old Town Newport with a view of the bridge.

After our showers, we cycled down a spiraling road that cut under the Conde McCollough Bridge. We quickly found ourselves along a river street replete with every kind of tavern, diner and art shop imaginable. Pungent fish odor punctuated the air. Barking seals raised a ruckus on the rocks near the harbor exit.

"Let's take a walk down by the fishing boats," said Sandi.

We placed our names on the waitlist and locked the bikes to the restaurant metal racks. The walk down to the big fishing rigs kept our rapt attention. Seagulls floated, soared and squawked all over the harbor. Out on the rocks, seals barked, yelped and complained to each other. Big fishing boats floated along the dock.

"This is really neat," said Sandi. "It feels like it felt 100 years ago. Those buildings are at least 120 years old. Generations of fishermen worked here. It's neat to see it."

After our tour, we stepped onto the second floor of the restaurant with a "wrap-around" glass view of the Conde McCollough Bridge spanning the harbor. During dinner, we watched the sun go down that yielded to a stunning pink sky. Pelicans flew across the horizon against that pink backdrop.

Next morning, we ate breakfast at the Beachfront Grill with seats looking out over the ocean. We watched seabirds, beachcombers and boats floating past the breakers.

Later, we pedaled the bikes over the McCollough Yaquina Bridge with spectacular cathedral spires rising upward like gallant Roman arches. The bridge consisted of green steel girders, millions of tons of cement and poetic designs in its infrastructure. Crossing it felt like riding over a piece of art.

For the rest of the day, we pedaled along the coast with not much to talk about. We snacked on endless blackberries that grew abundantly along Route 101. Near dusk, we asked a lady on the beach if we could camp on her lawn. She invited us to pitch our tent. In the morning, we looked out the tent flaps to see a pot of coffee, cups and bagels.

"I'll be darned," I said. "Yet another random act of kindness."

(Amazing wood carvings from shops along Route 101.
These humpback whales seemingly come alive.)

We packed up for a ride into a glorious day of sunshine. We pedaled along the crashing surf with diamonds sparkling across the waves. The road led up some 400-foot climbs until we reached Cape Perpetua where we saw the "Blue Hole": with a geyser that shot up 40-feet into the air with rough seas and big waves.

From there, we pedaled through deep woods to reach 400-feet of altitude and the "Devil's Churn" where the ocean crashed into a long lava trough until it smashed into the end of it. All along the West Coast ride, dramatic natural phenomena occurred daily. We coasted from Heceta Head in brilliant sunshine. In the tunnels, we pushed a button that set off a warning light system to let cars know that bikes rolled inside them. We clicked on our blinking red lights to make extra sure that everyone saw us coming and going.

After one downhill, we stopped on a bridge to see a fabulous 130-year-old lighthouse still operating. Below it, a pure white house gave the light keeper his abode. Lonely job!

(Blow hole erupting while a photographer waits for the geyser to explode.)

From the bridge, we pedaled 500 feet up to the Sea Lions Caves. However, none of them inhabited the caves that day because lots of food beckoned them into the ocean. We ate lunch at Nature's Café in Florence before heading out. We proceeded through deep green woods and massive clear cuts through mountainous terrain. The road offered stunning views.

We reached Reedsport where we devoured a fantastic pasta dinner at the Lighthouse Restaurant.

Next day, we pedaled up to the David Dewitt Memorial where we stopped to look at another Conde McCollough Bridge. Dewitt died in Vietnam. Several memorial plaques stated some powerful ideas: "The willingness with which our young people are willing to serve in any war no matter how justified, shall be directly proportional to how they perceive the veterans of earlier wars were treated and appreciated by their nation." President George Washington

Another plaque read, "There shall not be peace until the power of love overcomes the love of power." Latrine Wall, Pleiju, Vietnam 1968

We crossed that stunning bridge into North Bend. Once again, we pedaled over steel and concrete arches, elegant arcs and triangles that soared across the sky.

(Sandi standing before Dewitt Memorial just before crossing
a Conde McCollough Bridge on Route 101.)

At the visitor center, the lady suggested I run back under the bridge to see the intricate foundation of the bridge. While Sandi read all the information for restaurants, I treated myself to the underbelly of the Conde McCollough Bridge. What a fantastic experience!

During my picture-taking time, my kickstand bent after 20 years of use. Gratefully, when I pedaled back to the center, I stopped at Mo's Bicycle Shop to buy a new kickstand.

We pedaled toward Charleston along Route 101. As the sun faded, we pedaled down Seven Devils Road until we found a quiet campsite overlooking a huge tree-covered valley.

"Look, I really don't want to wax philosophic, but I will say that if you're alive, you've got to flap your arms and shake your legs, you've got to jump around a lot, you've got to make a lot of noise, because life is the very opposite of death." — Mel Brooks

Chapter 8

PLASTIC TRASH, ART, ETERNAL GLOAMING

Chapter 8: Thick fog, plastic trash turned into art, Great Pacific Garbage Patch, eternal gloaming

"Historians say that Leonardo da Vinci illustrated the first bicycle during his life during the Renaissance. His work along with many other artisans propelled Europe out of the Dark Ages. Once a chain drive took over, the bicycle became the most energy-efficient invention known to man. It challenged the entire transportation system, as it does today. The bicycle proves itself very inexpensive, incredibly reliable, uniquely healthy for the rider, and more so, it challenges as well as fascinates all of society. Along with its many benefits, it makes people happy. Oh my gosh! What a concept!" FHS

We awoke to sunshine and blue skies. We packed up and hit the road for a 20-mile ride of ups and down through deep woods fractured by clear-cuts.

We reached the quaint city of Bandon where we ate lunch at the natural grocery. Sandi stopped for an acupuncture appointment along with a chiropractor adjustment. I gave her a full body massage. The experience recharged her mind and body.

We followed the road into "Old Town Bandon." It featured a wharf with a jetty. The steel carcass of a huge ship protruded out of the sand near an ancient lighthouse. They cut the ship apart while making it a part of the jetty.

People stood on the dock throwing crab cages, loaded with chicken meat for bait, into the water. They dragged them up to throw back the females, but kept the males. Seagulls flew everywhere while pelicans glided over the waves out in the bay.

Every restaurant featured seafood in various dishes. The side streets offered endless art galleries, too!

(Seals play along every beach on the West Coast. They swim in the surf, lay on the rocks and frolic in sand. They enjoy the "good life.")

As we pedaled out of town, we accidently turned onto a street that carried us past a spectacular window display of plastic creatures created out of washed up plastic for 300 miles up and down the Oregon Coastline. The artist, Angela Pozzi, created an entirely new art form. We stepped inside to see all the plastic trash discarded in the Pacific Ocean that washed up on Oregon's coast. She fashioned it into plastic sharks, birds, seals and other collage items.

"Fascinating," said Sandi. "She teaches classes to high school students on the dangers of plastic trash in the oceans. Look at these sobering statistics. Incredibly sad."

(As you can see, discarded plastic components make up everything in this shark. From plastic shovel handles to Bic lighters to broken toys to plastic speakers that careless humans by the billions tossed into the oceans. It's pretty sickening to walk the beaches of the world and on many of them, I have walked in knee deep plastic. It makes a person want to scream in exasperation, but the leaders and the people of the world refuse to take action to stop it or clean it up.)

"Yeah, the Great Pacific Garbage Patch just 1,000 miles off the coast of San Francisco houses 100,000,000 (million) tons of floating plastic junk in a landmass the size of Texas," read a flyer. "It kills millions if not billions of marine and avian creatures annually."

Further information exposed that humans throw trillions of plastic bottles, soap containers, Styrofoam, toys, toothbrushes, fish netting, Bic lighters and more into the oceans without end. Some estimates show 2.5 million pieces of plastic tossed into our world's oceans 24/7. An astonishing 46,000 pieces of plastic float on every square mile of Earth's oceans.

We spent several hours watching other artists cement, paint and glue together plastic collages of plastic trash that 6,000 volunteers picked up along the Oregon Coast. While Pozzi brings a noble cause into the world, the only solution to humanity's trashing the oceans requires an international 50-cent deposit-return law on every piece of plastic container produced. Humans need financial incentives in order to save themselves from themselves.

"It's more than depressing," said Sandi. "Like there's no end to it as it only gets worse for all of the world's oceans."

"Roger that," I said. "Humans are clever, but not too smart. Let's get down the road."

As we pulled into Port Orford, the Pacific Ocean opened up with grand vistas revealing multiple rock islands offshore. The area featured aboriginal tribes that fished the area before being forced out of their homes and placed on reservations further north. Sadly, those reservations continue today. As the Indian lady said at the beginning of our trip, "You whites pulled the rug out from under us."

Miners, loggers and settlers polluted the rivers, killed the fish stocks and cleared the forests.

While it's painful to see what "progress" did to the area, we continued pedaling along Route 101 to Gold Beach that offered dramatic woods that opened up to vast beaches with eternal frothing waves pounding the sand and rocks.

The energy of the Pacific Ocean wafted over us with 20 mph tailwinds. Along the coast, footprints of beachcombers tracked everywhere into hidden coves, rocks and inlets. Gulls soared over the waves or stood in groups along the water line. Seals "surfed" the waves.

(Sandi rolling south on Route 101, West Coast, Oregon.)

Pedaling through such natural beauty creates a symbiotic physical, emotional and spiritual experience in us. As the wind blew, it moved across our bodies. It cooled us or it chilled us. While the sun shined, it warmed our faces and brightened our spirits. With the fog, we felt the dampness on our skin. With the rising of the sun in the mornings, the flowers awakened to their natural colors exploding from every meadow along our route. Coasting down hills yielded a wild flavor of joy to our child-like senses. Climbs brought disciplined determination. Through it all, the grand march of Mother Nature complimented us on our pedaling journey.

People like to travel. That is why the grass is greener over the fence. We are walkers – our natural means of travel is to put one foot in front of the other. The bicycle seduces our basic nature by making walking exciting. It lets us take 10-foot strides at 160 paces a minute. That's 20 miles an hour, instead of 4 or 5… It is not only how fast you go – cars are faster and jet planes faster still. But jet-plane travel is frustrating boredom – at least the car gives the pictorial illusion of travel. Cycling does it all – you have the complete satisfaction of arriving because your mind has chosen the path and steered you over it; your eyes have seen it; your muscles have felt it; your breathing, circulatory and digestive systems have all done their natural functions better than ever, and every part of your being knows you have traveled and arrived. **John Forester**

Chapter 9

TOOTHLESS MAN, CALIFORNIA

Chapter 9: Old man with toothless smile, the eternal ocean movement, difficult lives, coming into California

"Movement equates to the lifeblood of bicycling. You pedal through space and you travel through time. You ride on Earth's surface yet your pedals feather above terra-ferma in a kind of rhythmic dance. You press downward on the pedals, yet you drive the bike forward. It's an exchange of energy from your body to the steel beneath you. You transfer momentum from your legs to ultimately drive the rotation of the wheels. Those two metal rims wrapped in rubber become your wings. They will carry you around the world, if you choose. While you pedal, your eyes sweep the landscape before you. Birds catch your attention. Flowers delight you as they glisten in the morning sun. You carry an awareness of living as to the wind, sweat, heat, rain, cold and life-vibrations. Your mind ponders your existence or runs the gamut of your past history to your future plans. Or, you simply ride in a Zen-trance. You move into the morning until you pedal into the evening. At each point, the sun lights your path while life gallops along its own journey. You realize a wondrous connection to the natural world as you roll through it at 12-15 miles per hour. You might call it "the perfect

speed of life." Bicycling might be deemed one of the spiritual miracles of the universe." FHW

Every turn and curve on Route 101 featured endless rock islands anywhere from 50 to 200 yards out into the water. Some stood large as a barn. Others barely broke the surface. The road carved over the terrain like a giant Anaconda with no end in sight. Each time the highway crept closer to the ocean, we enjoyed those multifaceted islands featuring an array of seabirds perched on them whose waste turned the rocks white. Some birds flew in groups barely skimming the ocean surface. Others stood on the beaches alone or in bunches. We watched pelicans diving for fish. Always, a sense of life thriving with life.

Endless waves crashed over the rocks creating spectacular liquid fury. Chameleon skies painted a changing landscape against the Pacific's blue waters. With all the dramatic scenes before us, the journey remained enthralling, fascinating, gripping and visually spellbinding.

"That's an amazing sight," said Sandi. "It's like a painting, but it's living and moving with sparkling light and dancing waters until it becomes still in the distance on the horizon."

We crossed the highest viaduct in Oregon at the Thomas Creek Bridge that elevated 345 feet above the water. As usual, we plucked dozens of blackberries off their thorny bushes and popped them into our mouths.

(Sandi facing her demons along Route 101, West Coast, Oregon.)

Along the way, we ran into a 75-year old extremely thin man riding his dilapidated Fisher mountain bicycle. His panniers resembled a bagman in a big city. He appeared to be a homeless man on a bicycle. He wore a black stocking cap. When he smiled, no teeth. He dressed in ragged sweatpants with frazzled tennis shoes. His T-shirt hadn't seen a washing machine in months.

Yet, at 75 or older, with a scraggly gray beard, he smiled at the world. He laughed with us after making a silly joke. We offered him an apple, but he said he couldn't eat it on account of no molars to chew it. Instead, we gave him a Cliff Bar to "gum" until it softened with saliva and he could swallow it. After the energy bar, he called for a "group hug." We gave it to him. He represented a child with wonderment in his eyes. I slipped a $20.00 bill into his hand, "Enjoy a hot oatmeal breakfast with yogurt and bananas."

"You're so kind," he said.

I am amazed at what makes people happy with so little and people with so much to be so non-expressive and even unhappy. He looked so thin as to be emaciated; yet he pedaled his bike northward with a wave of his hand and twinkle in his eyes.

"You two be safe now," he said.

(Sandi stopped at a rest area in Port Orford with a
magnificent view along the Oregon Coast.)

In the next town, we stopped for treats at an ice cream store. While we waited, I turned around to see an extremely obese woman limping toward the ice cream counter while leading a blind lady. Two painful spirits struggling with life—barely able to walk to the counter for a treat. Then they struggled to get back out to their car. The heavy lady helped the blind lady into her seatbelt. Then, the lady struggled around the car and painfully labored to get into the front seat. It felt excruciating to watch.

Why were they chosen for such a difficult life experience? In my existence, I've seen the results of the Vietnam War with horrific wounds, dreadful burns and horrible PTSD. As a hospital medical tech, I saw the emergency ward overflow each day with traffic crash victims. You can be young, middle aged, rich, handsome, smart and educated—yet you may suffer severe bad luck in life. You can be born into good or bad circumstances, and for certain you will be confronted with many challenges in your life. If you're over the age of 60, you know what I'm talking about.

I know each day that I am alive, at 73, I am thankful, and I give thanks for my mental, emotional, physical and spiritual well-being. I am also aware that I could lose it at any moment to disease, tragedy, accident or otherwise.

And yet, during this delicious moment at Gold Beach, we watched a stunning sunset fall into the cloud soup. It rippled out to the right and left for miles.

Next day, we passed through Brookings along the coast. We pedaled until reaching the sign that read, "Welcome to California."

"Not too bad," said Sandi. "We're now in northern California. I can't wait to see the redwoods."

"Works for me, dear," I said.

Route 101 carried us through rolling hills, pastures, cows and horses. We rolled into Crescent City before reaching the Newton B. Drury Scenic Parkway.

We pulled into a www.WarmShowers.org rest stop at a church run by a lovely lady. There, we met Scott and Daniel. Scott, from Northern Michigan University, toured on a magnificent Kona mountain bike. He ran a bike shop through college. Daniel, a biologist from Konstanz, Germany, became our companion heading south in the morning.

From the rugged, colorful coastline of Oregon, the northern California coast brought a different flavor to our ride. Little did we know it, but that would change as we headed into the giant redwoods.

John Muir said it best, "The grand show is eternal. It is always sunrise somewhere; the dew is never dried all at once; a shower is forever falling; vapor is ever rising. Eternal sunrise, eternal dawn and gloaming, on sea and continents and islands, each in its turn, as the round earth rolls."

Chapter 10

CALIFORNIA AND MAJESTIC REDWOODS

Chapter 10: California, enormous redwoods, camping among 2,500-year-old trees

"Redwoods stand for centuries in defiance of 'Father Time'. They live for 2,500 years and longer. They drink 500 gallons of water daily as well as expire 500 gallons of water daily. They weigh 100 tons and more. They grow to a 25-foot diameter at the base. They survive fires, drought and disease. They have not survived humanity's ax as humans cut down 95 percent of them in the 1800's.

"Thankfully, a group of people saved them from total destruction back in 1900 with Save The Redwoods League. When you ride beneath their cathedral majesty, you feel like your bicycle gallops through 'time warriors' who stood while the Romans conquered the known world. They were 'old' when the Egyptians built the pyramids.

"Those quiet giants pierce the sky along the California coast like no other 'living beings' on Earth. At 360 feet tall, they stand like sentinels to the ages. To sit at the base of one of them means you 'feel' the historical energy of a tree that lived through 25 centuries of humanity's

fun and follies on this wondrous planet racing through the ink-black of the universe." FHW

We headed south along Route 101 until we reached a turn-off for the "Prairie Creek Redwood Grove".

"This will be one of the best treats of our entire West Coast ride," I said to Sandi and Daniel.

"Let's make it happen," said Sandi.

"I'm just along for the ride," said Daniel. "I've heard they are some pretty big trees."

Since I had traveled the coast as a 10-year-old kid with my parents, I saw them in my youth, teens, twenties, middle age and now into my golden years. With each visit, those gigantic trees stun me with their height, girth, weight, age and overall majesty. To ride through them bestows upon me such wonder and boggles my mind. To stand at the base of one of them captures my entire spiritual being. They carry me into a mystical trance of joy, appreciation and wonder.

We pedaled for another 20 minutes along rolling terrain until the road slipped quietly into the redwood grove. Each stand commands a name for whomever saved it from the lumberman's ax. Back in 1917, a group of Americans realized that 95 percent of the trees had been cut for fencing, homes, decks and shingles. Nobody at the time realized that redwoods took 2,500 years to grow. With only five percent left of the original trees, they formed the Save the Redwoods League. From that point to this day, private citizens donated money to buy all the remaining groves of redwoods. I became a member 30 years ago.

(Frosty, Sandi and Daniel at the base of a redwood in the Prairie
Creek Redwood Grove, California, West Coast Ride.)

For the next two hours, we pedaled through jaw dropping beauty in
the relative darkness of the forest floor. We stood beside redwoods, inside
burned out redwoods and walked on top of dead redwoods. We discovered
that when a redwood dies, it takes 20 to 30 years for it to fall over. It takes
up to 100 years for it to decay into the forest floor. Redwoods expire 500
gallons of water daily. They sport a base 25 feet in diameter.

Many of them grow in groups of four or five. To walk among them
feels like striding through a magical kingdom. Ferns grow everywhere
on the woodland floor. Lots of moss grows on dead trees. Lichens in all
colors decorate the forest grounds. Limbs and bark cover the forest floor.
Flowers of every kind peek out of the foliage. Birds chirp from all corners
of the redwood forest.

We stopped at one tree to take a picture of all of us spread across the
entire base with our bicycles. Another burned out tree, but still living,
housed three of our bikes and ourselves inside it for a picture. Another dead
tree, over 360 feet long, took us several minutes to walk its entire length.
The root systems measured 35-feet in diameter.

"This is beyond anything I've ever done," said Sandi. "I can't describe this kind of beauty."

"This must be the most beautiful forest I have ever seen," said Daniel.

"No question that this is 'jaw dropping awesome' beyond words," I said.

After our magical mystery tour through the Prairie Creek Redwood Grove, we stopped at the ranger station for lunch.

In the morning, we reached Trinidad, California where a fellow cyclist told us about the Hammond Trail hugging the coast. We took the route.

We weren't quite prepared for the extraordinary numbers of volcanic islands that hugged the shoreline. They created fantastic contrasts to the placid ocean.

(Sandi and Daniel standing inside a living, burned out redwood, California, West Coast Ride.)

We reached Arcata after blowing our minds with all the visuals.

We stopped into another WarmShowers couple, Dick and Kathie, who treated us to fresh honey, hot showers, warm dinner and fabulous hospitality. They invited us to stay over and share a potluck at the Grange House where a historian presented a fabulous slide show of the development of Humboldt County of Northern California.

Dick and Kathie proved themselves a Renaissance couple. They built their own home from scratch. Both bicycled around the world. He taught physics and she created crafts. He played the tuba. She painted. They both raised bees and sold honey. She created wise sayings on wood plaques.

We enjoyed no end to the marvelous kindness of strangers along our route. As we pulled out of Dick and Kathie's house, they took a shot of us to place in their two notebooks-full of touring cyclists from around the world.

We pedaled across long bridges that hovered over dry riverbeds. California stood in the middle of an extreme drought. As we rolled south, golden, dead grass dominated every mile of our ride. During our summer pedaling down the West Coast, we passed dozens of wildfires in Washington, Oregon and now into California.

California's 39 million people and headed toward 59 million within 30 years—need ever increasing amounts of water. As a man who has witnessed overpopulation around the world in places like China, India and other regions of the planet, I find our own country in serious denial of our predicament. Future generations face dramatic challenges on multiple fronts.

(Sandi and Daniel riding through the redwoods of California.
It was very peaceful with no traffic whatsoever.)

Chapter 11

CALIFORNIA AND AVENUE OF THE GIANTS

Chapter 11: Avenue of the Giants, a spiritual place of enormous beings

"That night, in the Avenue of the Giants, we cooked our food under 350-foot trees spanning 25 centuries. We looked up toward a starlit sky under which those trees grew for 2,500 years. Few contemplate the vastness of the universe because it's unfathomable. To live for 25 centuries slings a person's mind into confusion as to how those trees survived fires, droughts, floods, diseases and pestilence. No painting or photograph does them justice. A person cannot sense them by artificial means. By sleeping among them, we felt their antiquity. That night, we slumbered under a redwood canopy of spiritual eloquence replete with profound silence while we listened to the heartbeat of the universe in our dreams." FHW

Route 101 never disappoints. We stopped at a convenience store for water. On the side of the building, three guys reclined against a brick wall while a fourth man begged for money and food from shoppers. All four looked horribly dirty and disheveled.

I walked over, "Hey guys, I'm just an old guy, but I have a question for you."

"Shoot," said one of them.

"You are all young men," I said. "How come you struck out on the road without enough money to keep you fed? Why would you throw yourselves onto the financial mercy of others? Why didn't you take jobs, earn the money and then, travel?"

"We're free men," one said. "We don't work in an office and nobody bosses us around."

"Yes," I said. "But you accept money from people who work, pay their bills and are accountable to themselves."

"Yeah," another one said. "But they're not free; we are, so it's all a matter of choice."

"Travel in good health and high spirits," I said, realizing they lived in a different mindset.

(Sandi and Daniel riding along the Pacific Coast, Route
101, with endless rock islands out in the blue surf.)

Daniel and Sandi filled up their water bottles. We jumped on the bikes and sped south. You meet every kind of person on adventure highway. Each chooses his or her mode of travel. In the end, it's all good.

Later in the day, we exited the highway onto the "Avenue of the Giants" for yet another mystical, magical ride through one of the dozens of redwood groves saved by the www.SavetheRedwoodsLeague.org.

"Let's go see Founder's Grove where we can climb onto the Dyersville Giant," said Sandi. "It crashed in 1991, but it's the biggest tree at 367 feet tall, in these parts."

(One of the smaller redwoods along the Avenue of the Giants.)

Founder's Grove provides an ideal environment for big redwoods: it's on a large alluvial flat at the intersection of two rivers, shielded from storms by 3,000-foot-tall mountains to the west, yet still immersed in the summer fog that flows up the Eel River Valley. As a result, the grove has a lot of huge trees, but in addition it also has very large area and is relatively open, giving it an unusually expansive feel. These factors make the Founders' Grove one of the most impressive there is; it's really the quintessential redwood grove. Founder's Grove trail guide.

(The root system of a fallen giant engulfs Sandi in the
middle, West Coast Ride, Avenue of the Giants.)

For the next three hours, we hiked a 1.5-mile loop through burned out redwoods that still thrived in the mist that penetrated from the ocean. We took pictures from every angle. We climbed on massive dead trees. The Dyersville Giant provided over 120 yards of a wood pathway 20 feet off the ground. We played under a needle canopy that allowed very little light to hit the forest floor. While they live 2,500 years, it takes 20 to 30 years for a dead tree to fall and 100 years for it to decompose back into the forest floor. These trees grow taller than from the bottom to the top of Niagara Falls.

Later, we stopped at the Park Ranger's Visitor Center halfway through the grove. "Avenue of the Giants" runs for about 27 miles. One fellow, Charles Kellogg, built a truck out of a redwood tree to exhibit its enormous size. He toured the country in order to gain support for saving the last five percent of the redwoods. He imitated dozens of bird songs. He entertained and enthralled audiences for decades. His truck lives on in the visitor center.

That night, we pitched tents under the redwoods in the campgrounds. I can only describe the experience as deeply spiritual on more levels than I can explain.

The next day, we stopped dozens of times to take pictures of so many astounding trees and combinations of trees. If you carry a bucket list of things you want to accomplish in your lifetime, include the "Avenue of the Giants." There's nothing else on Earth that will spellbind you like giant redwoods.

Upon reflection of all my bicycle adventures around the globe from the Arctic to Antarctica, I've seen some amazing phenomena on this planet. I've crossed the Nullarbor Plains in the Australian Outback, hiked the Inca Trail, stood at the base of Mt. Everest, watched the sun never set in Alaska, faced grizzly bears in the Yukon Territory, scuba dived with sharks in the Galapagos Islands, stood on the Great Wall of China and a dozen other epic moments.

Those redwoods, well, they inspire me beyond this worldly realm. They captured a piece of my heart, mind and spirit. They live in me. Of all Nature's amazing creations, the redwoods dwell in my soul for my entire life. On my adventure memory shelf, I cherish a picture of my bike Condor and me in front of a big redwood painted in big letters, "Avenue of the Giants." I also enjoy a plastic bag filled with a redwood pine needles. I take note of those treasures every day I walk into my office to write. Bicycle adventure; it transports you into the universe.

As Sandi said, "This is a deeply spiritual place in the world."

Daniel added, "You could make that in the entire universe."

Chapter 12

UNIQUE MOMENTS IN OUR LIVES

Chapter 12: Leggett Hill, Coney Island Rollercoaster, deep woods, crashing waves of the Pacific Ocean

"Adventure creates unique "moments" for your heart, mind and body. You never forget the time when you slogged through a downpour along Oregon's coast. You remember that tornado funnel as you pedaled across Oklahoma. That special campfire under 14,000-foot peaks in Colorado stands out with shooting stars placing an exclamation point on your day. You remember that trip across Death Valley where you drank four gallons of water in one day, but never peed once. That evening of slumber beneath the 2,500-year-old Redwood giants touched your spirit beyond your imagination. You will always remember that night in the Sierras where Canadian geese dropped out of the sky for a final landing pad on the glass-still lake before you. Other ducks created V-wakes trailing behind them while diving ducks created circles. Ensconced in that magical scene, your campfire's embers enchanted you. While those moments abound on a bicycle adventure, the new day beckons you onward, not to tarry with yesterday—and, for you, another possibility for a unique 'moment' that will live in your body, mind and heart for the rest of your life." FHW

We ate breakfast with a melancholy mood from the knowledge that our time in the "Avenue of the Giants" slipped past with the coming of the day.

"I could ride through these trees every day for the rest of my life and still love every second of it," said Daniel.

"I've ridden through them a dozen times in my life," I said. "It's sad to leave, yet it's great to know they keep growing and thriving in the world no matter what humanity does to itself."

"This is truly a remarkable kingdom of trees," said Sandi. "I've got to come back again."

We passed out of the park around noon. The road continued through small towns like Miranda, Redway, Garberville, Piercy and ended up at Standish-Hickey State Park.

Hot showers work wonders on a man's and woman's soul! We basked in three minutes of steaming, liquid joy. Ah, to be clean! Refreshed!

As we cooked dinner, three other cyclists stopped in for the night. One guy pedaled a light framed road bike. He said he saw me earlier in the day and didn't like my heavy rig.

He noted, "You're too heavy, too much weight, dude."

I said, "Everybody's got to follow their own style. Why two different rims?"

"Oh, my 32-spoke rim collapsed on me," he said. "But it's still better than riding a heavy mountain bike."

"Have at it," I said. "You've got to make yourself happy!"

I quickly noticed all three dudes delighted in their alternative universe from smoking doobies.

(The simplest events bring the biggest smile to your face while
on bicycle tour. So often, our silent mode of travel surprises
wild critters out doing their own thing. Wonderful!)

In the morning, we cooked breakfast, packed and hit the road by 9:00
a.m. Just down the highway, we turned off to ride our bikes through a
hole in a living redwood large enough to allow passage of cars. After a few
pictures, we quickly reached Leggett where we began a 2,500-foot climb
into deep woods. The road snaked up through hundreds of curves in the
next 10-miles of climbing. For two hours we climbed in Granny gear at 6
to 8 percent grade. We averaged four miles per hour.

Not hard, relatively speaking, because of our physically tuned legs, but
steady pedal work. We listened for cars coming up the hill behind us to
make sure we didn't get caught in compromising situations with no place
to pull out. There's nothing worse than riding around a blind curve with
another car or truck coming behind and one in front. If they pass at your
location, it's a distressing situation.

At the same time, pedaling through dense wilderness like that, you
settle into a rhythm. Time ceases to make a difference. You don't think

about the top until you reach it. Unlike high multi-switchback mountain passes where you can see the top, in the woods, it's all-immediate.

Near noon, we reached the summit. Daniel waited for us. I knew he would rather go faster, but he liked Sandi's and my company. He'd been riding alone for several months. I could relate to the feeling of loneliness from solo touring. He gave up a little time for fellowship with a couple old enough to be his parents, and actually, I'm old enough to be his grandfather. It's funny, because I don't feel any age while riding my bicycle. I feel like a kid.

At the top, we guzzled water from our bottles. We slipped into our nylon jackets. In seconds, we raced down our own 10-mile Coney Island rollercoaster ride with thrills and chills. Green trees, golden underbrush and fresh pavement with a double yellow line—made for one heck of a "yahoo" ride down that hill. Just thrilling! Exhilarating! Fun! Fun! Fun!

At the bottom, the road inclined into another 1,000-foot climb through deep woods. We felt so energized that we didn't feel the "hardship" of the long pull upward. Relatively quickly, we once again descended into another wild ride to the ocean.

Without notice, we coasted up to a big curve with nothing but sky ahead of us. Within seconds, we pulled the bikes over to see the eternal waves crashing on the rocks 300 feet below us.

"Wow," said Sandi. "That was the greatest bicycle ride of my life. More fun than Disneyland!"

"I never expected such a curvy road," said Daniel. "That was a ton of fun."

In front of us, black volcanic islands dotted the ocean near the shore. Sea birds flew everywhere around the rocks. Waves crashed on the beaches and turned to water white where they crashed on the islands. Fresh Pacific Ocean air blew into our lungs like an energy bolt.

"You can't help but realize how infinitely tiny each of us is in contrast to this planet," said Daniel, a biologist. "Just looking out at this ocean makes me realize how infinitesimally small anyone of us is when looking at the universe."

"Kind of blows me away, too," I said. "There's no way to figure out the universe, so we just have to reckon how to navigate our time on this planet for our lives. Past that, it's potluck and one big mystery."

"The key," said Sandi. "Let's enjoy it while we've got it in our hands."

(Eating dinner with new friends at a www.warmshowers.org stop along Route 101. That's Frosty, Daniel, Jack, Scott and Sandi.)

Chapter 13

YOU NEVER KNOW ABOUT THE ROAD OF LIFE

Chapter 13: Robin Williams, Bodega Bay and The Birds, Alfred Hitchcock's horror movies, ironies of life.

"Your life on a bicycle begins with you in the saddle, pressing your thighs into the pedals, moving into the morning sunshine, sweating in the heat of the day, climbing the next hill and guzzling from your water bottle. Trail mix crunches around your teeth. "Chase and catch" the things you love in life. When you follow that path, your best friends appear. They cannot help but be drawn to your energy, your smile and your countenance. Your "high-spoke" vibrations attract the noblest and brightest along life's highway. Share your dream with another cyclist. Ask about theirs. Get lost in the heat of the day while you pedal into that sweet spot in the afternoon when the air cools to match that flawless moment of perfection—your bicycle Zen: you ride your bicycle because you love to ride your bicycle. Life beckons you to live your dreams and wear your passions with a smile." FHW

We covered 65 miles with endless dramatic ocean views and million-dollar summer homes of rich San Franciscans. The road curled 300-feet above the surf until it dove dozens of times around steep curves to carry us down to the coves along the beaches. Quickly, the road wound back toward the sky.

Each descent took less than 60 seconds while each climb took 10 to 20 minutes. We chilled, and then sweated with each event of the coves, surf and sand. Near dusk, we felt exhausted from all the climbing and descending throughout the day. We reached Sea Ranch for a stop in a wooded grove and a nice hot dinner.

From Sea Ranch to Bodega Bay, the road snaked for endless miles across coves. In each cove, trailers and campers flooded the areas to create a small community.

The closer we traveled to San Francisco, the more dramatic the homes. Whomever makes that kind of money, they excel at building Pacific Ocean castles. No doubt they witness stunning sunsets on a regular basis.

We continued enjoying breathtaking vistas and huge islands out in the surf. We stopped in Bodega Bay in the late afternoon where potato salad ran $8.99 a pound. Obviously a very expensive tourist town! We stopped at a gift shop with posters of movie stars such as Marilyn Monroe, Clark Gable and Clint Eastwood.

(Stopping for lunch along Route 101 with Sandi and Daniel.)

Bodega Bay remains famous for horror movie director Alfred Hitchcock's "The Birds" with Tippi Hedren and Rod Taylor. She visits the Bay once a year to sign autographs for her book.

At the time, Hitchcock demanded her affections, but she rebuffed him. He told her he would ruin her career if she didn't bed him. She remained resolute. Sure enough, he blacklisted her in Hollywood and she never starred again. She wrote about it in her memoirs. Hitchcock and Harvey Weinstein may share much in common.

Sandi walked into the visitor's office to get directions. A few minutes later, she hurried out yelling, "You won't believe who died."

"Who?" asked Daniel.

"Yeah, who?" I asked.

Crying, she said, "Robin Williams."

"Oh my God," I said. "How?"

"Suicide," Sandi said.

"Oh, that makes me sick," I said.

"Yes, we know Robin Williams in Germany," said Daniel. "He's world famous and rich, so why would he kill himself?"

"He struggled with alcohol, drugs and depression," I said.

"So sad," said Sandi.

During this lifetime, the craziest events often occur without reason. Tragedy befell Elvis Presley, Marilyn Monroe, Ray Charles, Lou Gehrig and James Dean—all rich and famous. Some of the most boring people live into their 90's. The rich come and go. The poor exist in oblivion. No rhyme. No reason. No understanding of why.

(Marilyn Monroe still fires the imaginations of men and women
50 years after her death. Her famous shot with air blowing
up from the vent may last into the centuries ahead.)

We discovered that Robins' hung himself because he suffered from extreme depression. Some suggested he faced Parkinson's Disease and didn't want to become a cripple. No matter what the reason, his daily life became more painful than death.

Williams' death hit me like a boulder falling on my emotional head because four of my friends died in April of this year. They died of cancer and heart attacks. One day I talked with them and the next, I attended their memorials. I spread the ashes of one of my friends at the top of a 14,000-foot peak in Colorado. I cried my eyes out as I spread his ashes to the four winds of the universe.

Like millions of people, I loved Robin Williams from his hit TV comedy, "Mork and Mindy", to his movies, his charity work and his "thriving" in the world. Who can forget "Mrs. Doubtfire" or "Dead Poet's Society" or "Good Morning Vietnam"?

One thing about aging: you mourn the deaths of your friends and family. And, one day, you know your time on this planet faces a departure date. That's why we keep pedaling so old age can't catch up so quickly.

After securing our foodstuffs, we pedaled over to the state park with showers and campground for "Hiker-bikers."

Sitting on the picnic table that night, we cooked dinner on our one-burner stove. A flock of seagulls dropped out of the sky looking for handouts. The sun sank into the ocean with the subtleness of a thief slipping into the night. Out in the water on the rocks, dozens of seals barked at the coming of the night.

For me, I slipped into the tent with great appreciation for still being alive. I get to see another sunrise. I get to hug Sandi.

I get to meet new people tomorrow. Like I said, "Life is short. Live your dreams and wear your passions with a smile."

Chapter 14

GOLDEN GATE BRIDGE

Chapter 14: Elephant seals, drought, Stinson Beach, San Francisco, Golden Gate Bridge, Tony Bennet

"Pedaling up a mountain means sweat, sweat and more sweat! Muscle and blood! Gumption and determination! True grit! It takes a certain gut level of "stubborn joy" when cycling up a long grade. For certain, no one else will pedal for you. Granny gear allows you to "spin" fast, but go slowly. Your mind evolves into a mental tenacity with one purpose— to reach the top. Arriving at the crest yields a certain elation and/or pleasure to every cell in your body. You "feel" the wonder of the quest. Gradually, you feel gravity-powered downhill bliss. It doesn't get any better than that! Less than a billionth of a percent of humans tour the world on a bicycle. But for you who ride, you experience the incredible mental, physical and spiritual renaissance your body, mind and spirit experience beyond the normal humdrum of life lived by most human beings. My bet: you wouldn't trade it for a Rolls Royce." FHW

Up in the morning to more wind, cold and fog. I see why northern California lacks a lot of population growth.

We pedaled to Pt. Reyes where we enjoyed a large Elephant Seal colony. Seal killers hunted them to near extinction back in the 1800's, but they recovered from a tiny group of 150 to 150,000 in 2018. Today, they remain on the "Endangered Species" list.

Ironically, on average, 250 species suffer extinction in the 48 contiguous states of America, annually, according to the Department of the Interior. Many suffer extinction before officials place them on the Endangered Species list. All of it caused by human encroachment on animal habitat, toxic poisons and disruption of their food chain.

From Pt. Reyes, we pedaled south through long uphill and downhill canyons lined with eucalyptus trees. The road incessantly climbed and dropped through farm fields with cows grazing on brown, dead grass.

California faces horrific drought and fires. I am amazed the trees don't die off in mass. Later, I discovered forest rangers estimated that 12 million trees died off from lack of water in one year. It's unsettling to think that California expects to add 20 million people within 30 years. At that juncture, their water shortages won't find a solution. I witnessed the same difficulties in my world travels in Asia, Mexico and South America. Humans stretch Nature to the limit by exceeding its carrying capacity—then wonder why they suffer starvation because they can't feed and water themselves.

We pedaled along the beach to enjoy seagulls, ducks and cormorants. Entering the tiny surfing town of Stinson Beach, I noticed the road entered the town, then immediately climbed a 2,500-foot mountain.

"Looks like we pay a price before dinner tonight," said Daniel.

"We have to do it," said Sandi, "if we expect to reach our Warmshowers host before nightfall."

"Let's do it," I said.

We climbed 1,000 feet over multiple switchbacks until we dove back down 1,000 feet to ride by John Muir Woods. Again, the road began another climb of 2,000 feet.

"Holy catfish," I said.

"What does that mean?" asked Daniel.

"Exasperation," I replied. "That's a hell of a climb at the end of a long day."

"We must do it," Daniel said.

"Yes, I'm hungry," said Sandi. "Let's get over the top."

I slipped my feet into the pedals, leaned forward and began to sweat. The road climbed up to the sky. Hundreds of cars passed us. We rolled at four mph for the next hour with some 12 percent grades that tested every muscle in our bodies.

Pedaling up a mountain: sweat, sweat, sweat! Muscle and blood! Blood and muscle! Gumption and determination! It takes a certain gut level "never say die" kind of attitude when cycling up a steep grade. For certain, no one else will pedal for you.

Granny gear allows you to "spin" fast, but go slowly. Your mind evolves into a mental tenacity with one purpose—to reach the top. But for you who ride, you grasp the incredible mental, physical and spiritual renaissance your body, mind and spirit experience beyond the normal day of life lived by most human beings.

At the top, excitement grabbed us. Only 30 minutes to Doug's house, hot shower and vegetarian meal prepared by a vegetarian chef in Sausalito who live right next to the Golden Gate Bridge.

We flew down the side of the mountain, but suddenly, Daniel's brakes faded. Luckily, he stopped the bike with what little braking power was left on his brake pads.

"Let's adjust them before you kill yourself," I said.

Daniel hadn't checked his brakes and he could have paid for his mistake with his life. I am amazed he stopped the bike. His brake levers plunged to a stop against the handlebars.

I adjusted front and back brakes to give him plenty of braking power. I cleaned his rims of oil to give a better grip. One rear brake pad wouldn't snap back from the rim, but I couldn't figure out the problem.

"Man, you gotta' use a cloth to clean your rims every day so your brake pads can grip to stop you," I said. "We need to stop by a bike shop in the morning to check your brakes."

"Thanks," he said. "I won't forget that lesson."

We rolled into Sausalito along a river. Soon, we reached the main drag of town where million-dollar sailboats floated in their slips. One boat resembled the Taj Mahal. That's what you can do when you enjoy a lot of time and money.

"I am famished," said Sandi.

"Me too," said Daniel.

We proceeded along the heavy thoroughfare to reach Turney Street where Doug greeted us with open arms. He rode across America coast-to-coast as well as Canada-to-Mexico. He also organized day rides to Stinson Beach and back.

Surprisingly, we discovered that we both graduated from Michigan State University. Wow! Who woulda' thunk it?

Doug created a delicious salad, veggie lasagna and cheesecake dessert smothered in strawberry sauce. He followed it with chocolate cookies and homemade sorbet.

"You folks want to see the sunset over Golden Gate Bridge?" said Doug.

"You bet," Daniel said.

(Golden Gate Bridge at sunset over the San Francisco Bay.
Stunning combination of lights, water and sky.)

Doug drove us up to a big lookout point overlooking the entire San Francisco Bay along with the Golden Gate Bridge. As the sun settled into the Pacific Ocean, the lights of the bridge twinkled and the entire bay lit up with boats, skyscrapers and moving cars over the Golden Gate and Bay Bridge.

"Boy, this is some sight," Daniel said.

In the morning, we bid adieu to Doug with tremendous thanks for his hospitality. I am always thankful for the kindness of strangers.

"Let's get into San Francisco," I said. "The Golden Gate Bridge awaits you."

"I'm excited about pedaling over such an historic bridge," said Sandi.

We checked into a bicycle shop along the strip to see what we could see with Daniel's brakes. I felt he needed an extra pair of eyes to discover the problem. At the shop, the mechanic took one look to see a clip that pulled the brakes back off the rim—totally not adjusted into place. He snapped it back onto a hook and the brakes operated correctly on the back wheel.

"Now, you've got two good brakes," I said.

We pedaled up the hill to the Golden Gate Bridge viewing stand. From the North side, we looked down on the cars crossing and people walking on the sides. It's an amazing piece of engineering for 1937.

- 83,000 tons of concrete
- 80,000 miles of cables, equates to three times around the Earth at the equator
- 16 years to build

We snapped pictures, talked to dozens of tourists and finally, pedaled our bikes across the bridge. On my I-pod, Tony Bennett sang, "I left my heart in San Francisco, high on a hill, it calls to me…to be where little cable cars…climb halfway to the stars…the morning fog may chill the air, I don't care, my love waits there in San Francisco…above the blue and windy sea…when I come home to you San Francisco, your golden sun will shine for me."

(Constant wildlife greeted us around every corner
of the road along the West Coast.)

Chapter 15

CITY BY THE BAY, SAN FRANCISCO

Chapter 15: San Francisco, Lombard Street, trolley cars, Fisherman's Wharf

"Bicycling unites physical harmony coupled with emotional bliss to create a sense of spiritual perfection that combines one's body, mind and soul into a single moving entity. You, the cyclist, power your steel steed with two spoked metal rims wrapped in rubber tires toward the distant horizon. That far-off place where the sky meets the earth, holds promise on multiple levels. Bicycling allows you to mesh with the sun, sky and road in a special dance with the day, with the moment, with friends or with your own far-off adventure fantasies. At the perfect speed, you flow unerringly toward your destiny. In fact, all your worries, cares and troubles vanish in the rear-view mirror while you bicycle along the highways of the world: you pedal as one with the Nature." FHW

Pedaling a fully-loaded bicycle over the Golden Gate Bridge moved our spirits in ways we couldn't have imagine. At first, we stood on the north side of the viewing area. Speeding traffic crossed the "orange" bridge in both directions. People walked on the east side of the bridge with dozens of them taking pictures or staring downward to the choppy waters below. Out to the west, the blue Pacific faded into the horizon.

"Nice day with no fog rolling into Frisco Bay," I said to Daniel.

"Yes, I'm told the fog covers the bridge much of the time," said Sandi.

Looking at the bridge commands your eyes to the enormity of the cables and steel works that form its grandeur. If you look at bridges around the world in the 21st century, they provide stunning architecture, but the Golden Gate's fame spans the entire world. Everyone from every country wants to walk across the bridge on the "City by the Bay."

We rolled over the bridge slowly, pausing to snap numerous pictures. After a half hour, we reached the other side where a souvenir shop sold everything from miniature bridges to baseball caps. All made in China, of course!

From there, we pedaled along the bay until we reached Fisherman's Wharf. Vendors sold paintings, trinkets, three-minute profiles of your face, T-shirts and necklaces. Tourists waited in long lines for a ride on the famed cable cars that carried them up extremely steep roads interconnecting the city.

We secured the bikes to walk on Pier 39 where we saw break dancers, steel drum players, guitarists, mimes, jugglers and human statues. Everybody hustled for money.

(San Francisco's famous cable cars carrying tourists
all over the rugged hills of the city.)

(Daniel riding down the curviest road in the world: Lombard Street,
famous for many movie car chase scenes with Steve McQueen.)

Later in the morning, we pedaled to the top of Lombard Street, famous
for being the curviest street in the world. Many movie chase scenes for the
past 60 years raced around the curves of Lombard Street. Steve McQueen,
in "Bullitt", careened through the curves in his Ford Mustang. Of course,
we maneuvered our bikes down that cobbled street, too. You can't have
too much fun on a bicycle tour.

Late in the day, we sat down at a sandwich shop for our last conversation.
We advised Daniel to visit Yosemite National Park. Sandi and I would
continue southward on the Pacific Coast Highway Route 1.

(Street bands, dancers, artists, jugglers, mimes, trinket salespersons
and much more inhabit Fisherman's Wharf in San Francisco to
the delight of everyone who visits the "City by the Bay.")

We hugged. We cried. We told him what a fine young man his
parents brought into the world. It's fascinating how we become so attached
emotionally to another cyclist. It's our nature.

Sandi and I pedaled south on Route 1 until twilight. A man named
Robert yelled out at a stop light, "I pedaled coast to coast back in 1990."

"Fantastic," Sandi said. "You know we're having fun. Hey, any chance
you could direct us to a campground around here?"

"Yes, you can camp in my back yard," he said. "Follow me."

We followed him six blocks to his house with the perfect back yard
for a tent. Robert brought out his two boys to share a plate of apples and
pears along with cheese. We learned that his wife died of cancer when the
boys reached five and six years of age. He raised both sons by himself.
Both became honor students and track stars. Plus, they sang in a choir
that toured the world.

"I'm so proud of you young men," I said. "I lost my father when I was young, and you lost your mother. But you know something, you will go forward to live great lives."

They seemed delighted that I talked directly to them. They gave Sandi and me a firm handshake, which showed us a solid sense of integrity. And, they looked us in the eyes. I appreciate that in a person when we meet.

Up at dawn, we folded the tent, deflated our sleeping mattresses and rolled up our sleeping bags. We left a nice note, and sped south along Route 1.

We sent Robert and his sons ten of my "Spirit of Adventure" greeting cards when we returned home—just a little thanks for their kindness.

We powered through incessant traffic along the coast. Endless gridlock and horns! Surfers waited for waves along the coast for their 10 seconds of riding. I like windsurfing myself so I can keep flying around the water without waiting for the next big wave. Kite boarders seem to be coming ever more popular because they can ride waves via the wind all day long.

The coast provided us with ascents and descents throughout the day. Sunny weather. Blue Pacific waters.

I also noticed that California's demographics changed since I traveled three west to east tours and three coast tours in the past 40 years. Endless gridlocked traffic! It's changed from European-Americans to predominantly Asian, Chinese, Indian, Mexican and African immigrants.

Heading south, dramatic ocean views with cliffs and rugged islands dotted the waters. Seabirds flew everywhere and nested on the rock islands.

Along the way, we passed hundreds of cars stuck in gridlocked traffic.

(Sun sinking into the Pacific Ocean. We camped out on a cliff
to watch it finish off the day with sublime beauty.)

Chapter 16

MONTEREY AQUARIUM AND BIG SUR

Chapter 16: Cannery Row, John Steinbeck, Pebble Beach, multi-million-dollar homes

"Riding a bicycle flat-out brings joy throughout your mind, body and spirit. Pedaling scintillates every cell in your being toward some kind of nirvana, state of grace and/or total euphoric bliss. Of course, not every second, yet when it arrives, you 'fly' at the perfect speed. It might be deemed something like the ancients equate to enlightenment. Some call it the perfect connection with Nature: eudemonia. It means you become a seeker of spirit, of joy and of spiritual energy. Whatever you call it, the feelings ring from the rafters of your mind. Your eyes dance with delight. Your nostrils flare with amazing scents wafting in the breeze. Your skin absorbs the energy of the wind, rain and stars. Everyone enjoys that smile on your face and in your spirit when they meet you on your bicycle tour." FHW

The ride along the coast south of San Francisco featured a strange "house" perched upon a cliff overlooking the Pacific Ocean. Our military built it as a big canon bunker to repel any attacks during WWII. Nevertheless, it remains as a strange relic of humanity's need to build something ugly, and then, leave it there to degrade through millions of years.

"Why don't they bulldoze that ugly pile of concrete?" said Sandi.

"It's always curious to me why Americans tout the beauty of America from "sea to shining sea", but discard their vehicles, buildings and entire towns into the wilderness in every state, to degrade over the next million years. We are incredibly irresponsible toward the natural world. I don't see it changing, but in fact, becoming worse over the years."

(Sandi headed southbound on Route 101 of the Pacific Coast Highway.)

The road dissected fields of crops such as strawberries, celery and cauliflower. We passed numerous fruit stands along the route.

At Marina, we met a fellow cyclist who pulled a two wheeled bugger cart behind him. He hauled more junk than a big city bagman pushing a grocery basket. He pedaled a lonely highway on his singular journey. We've met such travelers in our journeys around the planet. They live solitary lives, much like hobos that ride trains. We're not sure what causes such a life, but we're thankful for our lottery ticket in life. But for the grace of luck and our good fortune, we enjoy our adventures—and then go home to hearth, home and friends.

Upon reaching Monterey, the focal point stands around statues in Cannery Row. That's where Californians first began canning sardines. John Steinbeck earned a Nobel Prize in literature for his novels such as **Grapes of Wrath**, but also wrote touching travel stories like **Travels with Charlie: In Search of America.**

"When I was very young and the urge to be someplace else was on me, I was assured by mature people that maturity would erase this itch. When years described me as mature, the remedy prescribed was middle age. In middle age I was assured greater age would calm my fever and now that I am fifty-eight perhaps senility will do the job. Nothing has worked. Four hoarse blasts of a ship's whistle still raise the hair on my neck and set my feet to tapping. The sound of a jet, an engine warming up, even the clopping of shod hooves on pavement brings on the ancient shudder, the dry mouth and vacant eye, the hot palms and the churn of my stomach high up under the rib cage. In other words, once a bum always a bum. I fear this disease is incurable." John Steinbeck, **Travels with Charley: In Search of America**

We snapped a few pictures of the statues of Steinbeck and his friends in Cannery Row. Monterey Bay, replete with mesmerizing blue waters, stretched into the Pacific Ocean. Kayakers, sailboats, wharf posts and seaweed decorated the waters. Seagulls glided on updrafts. Piers, which housed tourist businesses of every kind, jutted out from shore.

(John Steinbeck atop this rock accompanied by his friends
in Cannery Row. Monterey Bay offers tourists everything
from a sea aquarium to Pebble Beach Golf Course.)

At the end of the street, we locked our bikes Gracie and Condor to a
flagpole, and walked up to the booth for the Monterey Aquarium. They
charged a dear price at $39.00 for admission, yet hundreds lined up to see
the show.

As a lifelong scuba diver, I love everything under the surface. It's
magical under the waves with all the sea creatures of the world. Everything
moves in slow motion. Everything works in balance.

Inside that aquarium, we enjoyed hammerhead sharks, reef sharks,
tuna, sea otters, jellyfish, boxfish and dozens of other sea creatures. They
featured a "wave room" where simulated waves crashed over the guests.
They offered a penguin colony.

Additionally, they featured a marvelous movie about the oceans. They
showed how we are destroying the seas and marine life with discarded
plastics and poisons. Several artists created birds and sharks from plastic
debris. Sickening and sad, if not enough to make anyone angry at our
disregard for the oceans!

They noted that humans created the "Great Pacific Garbage Patch" about 1,000 miles off San Francisco. It's loaded with 100 million tons of plastic with depths from 30 to 60 feet deep and the size of Texas. It kills millions of sea and avian creatures annually. It loaded with every kind of plastic debris that humans toss into the oceans: plastic bags, Bic lighters, toothbrushes, baby diapers, toys, Styrofoam packing, garbage bags and 1,000 other plastic items of all descriptions.

Marine creatures eat the plastic and die from having their guts blocked up. Whales and dolphins die along with sharks, seals and so many other creatures. Same with birds who eat bottle caps and die from stuffed-up guts. Worse, humans toss 2,500 more pieces of plastic into the oceans 24/7. A simple 50 cent deposit-return international law on all plastics would solve it, but no world leaders will speak up for such a common-sense law. The kids of the world would find a new job and purpose with such a law.

One exhibit showed how our fossil fuel burning carbon exhaust warms the oceans and creates acidity, which destroys marine habitat, kills reefs around the world, and causes the extinction of untold numbers of marine creatures.

On a lighter note, they featured inventions founded on the shapes and techniques that birds and fish utilize to stay alive.

(Rather large octopus looks visitors in the eyes as if he were asking, "Why did you take me out of my ocean home and stick me behind this glass?")

A King Fisher's beak and body dive into the water without a splash. Engineers utilized the exact same shape for the nose of high-speed trains in Europe to stop the explosion created when they entered and exited tunnels at 200 miles per hour.

A shark never suffers barnacles, but a whale grows them like flowers on its skin. Scientists found out that sharks' skin consists of "shingles" that don't allow barnacles to gain a grip. Thus, all ships today enjoy the same concept to stop barnacles and reduce drag, which saves billions of dollars and gives greater fuel efficiency.

All in all, we enjoyed a fabulous morning with octopus exhibits, whales and dolphins.

(Jellyfish create astoundingly intricate patterns and movement.
You can't help asking yourself, "Why did nature and how did
nature create something like this creature…and for what?")

We pedaled out of Monterey along the famous Pebble Beach Golf Course. Man, oh man, talk about exceedingly rich folks living in multi-million-dollar homes! Money drips from every Mercedes, BMW, Ferrari and Lamborghini that passed us.

The road led us to 17-Mile Drive, which featured endless wealthy homes on the ocean. We couldn't help wondering how those people gained such incredible wealth. How do they do it? Do they work like the rest of us? How do they live? What makes them different from 95 percent of Americans struggling to pay their mortgages? Then, when we considered that billions of people live wretched lives planet-wide, it was all the more disheartening. This fact remains: life isn't fair.

That night, we camped at Big Sur State Park just before entering Big Sur, the legendary road that snakes along high cliffs to give cyclists spectacular views of coastline. We were informed that cyclists cannot pedal slowly enough to absorb all the beauty.

Chapter 17

THE MAGIC OF BIG SUR

Chapter 17: Stunning vistas, whales, otters, sea lions, sea birds

"The stretch of serpentine highway south of Monterey Bay, California known as the Big Sur, creates a dynamic collision of cliffs and waves of the Pacific Ocean on the West Coast of America. You sweat while climbing its serpentine ridges. You yell with delight while screaming down its raging descents. As a cyclist, you stand with your mouth agape at every vista stop where the ocean collides with the rocky cliffs. White sand beaches and waterfalls mesmerize not only your eyes, but they inspire the very best of your humanity. You might watch a line of 10 pelicans flying in formation above the surf. At other times, you watch dolphins surfing the waves. Out there in that wide, blue Pacific Ocean, a Gray whale exhales a 15-foot spray upon surfacing. A moment later, you might watch a sea otter rolled over on its back as it lunches on an abalone. At some point, you touch the waves, and at others, you fly 1,000 feet above the surf. All in all, the Big Sur etches its grandeur into your thighs while carving memories into your adventure to last a lifetime." FHW

Have you ever awoken one day on your own adventure not imagining what you faced? Have you ever climbed a mountain only to be confronted by a bear? Did you crack out of your tent to see a stunning sunrise on Mt. Everest? What happened on that canoe trip in January in Michigan on the Pine River when you caught a log and fell into icy waters? I did and froze half to death, resulting in double pneumonia. How about riding into a 10-inch snowstorm in the Andes at 15,000 feet? What about scuba diving with sharks in the Galapagos Islands? You never know what to expect on an adventure. How do you define it?

(The Big Sur of California's coastline features dramatic cliffs, ocean waves crashing on islands, seabirds, seals, whales, otters, dolphins and dramatic scenery.)

One thing you may remember about any quest: adventure may not always be comfortable, but it's still adventure.

We woke up to birds squawking in the trees and the sound of waves crashing on the beach. Seagulls bickered with one another while pelicans glided over the crest of waves. We stretched, cooked breakfast, pulled up the tent, and packed the gear.

For the entire morning, we cranked up 1,000-foot cliffs only to descend back down to 300 feet. The blue Pacific Ocean waters sparkled like trillions of diamonds. Aspirin-white waves crashed onto sandy beaches.

Every kind of bird flew in every kind of formation. The road resembled a thin snake with no end as it slithered around every contour of the terrain.

At one moment, we traveled through dense woods and just as suddenly, upward along a barren rock cliff. Out in the water, rock islands featured hundreds of birds such as cormorants, pelicans and seagulls. Otters slapped their flippers as they floated on their backs. Seals played in the surf.

(Elephant seals sleeping by the thousands, stacked up on each other, flipping sand on their backs and barking for no apparent reason other than letting others know they are alive.)

The stunning scenery around us made the pedaling incidental. It felt like when those kids rode with E.T. across the full moon. A feeling swept over us like we were riding through a dream. We pedaled an elegant serpent meandering on the wings of the Pacific Ocean.

Some call it "satori" while others call it "Zen". Many feel an almost drug-like "high" racing through their systems. The Greek philosopher Aristotle spoke about it in his **Nicomachean Ethics** book. He attempted to define happiness.

Essentially, he said that human happiness is not so much an outcome or end-state, but a realization of one's true nature. Or, fulfilling one's potential and living with a sense of daily joy. That certainly describes bicycle touring or even day-rides on your steel fun-machine.

In one sense, in this highly complex world, many of us yearn for simpler lives, less stressed lives and more tranquil lives. A bicycle tour brings out the very essence of "Zen" in that you engage several basic needs in life: eat, pedal, sweat, sleep, explore and live creatively. Past that, the world breaks other peoples' hearts, but for this moment in your life, you enjoy the pure daily joy of living.

The Big Sur creates gnarly, mystical energy that flies out of your body, onto the pedals and into the wild blue yonder. You stop to gasp at the beauty at every ocean point vista overlook. Of all the wonders of the West Coast of America, the Big Sur captures your youth to leave memories for your lifetime.

Arduous climbs become triumphs for your spirit while the downhill roller-coaster rides cause every cell in your body to cheer with euphoria. You yell in sheer delight while you charge into another sunlit blue-sky curve.

At one vista point about 150 feet above a deep lagoon, we stopped for a drink. A lady sat on the rocks pointing out something to her husband who stood behind a tripod with a 1,000 mm camera lens.

"There she blows," the lady said, pointing.

We looked down to see a 30-ton Gray whale and her baby calf surface out of the greenish-blue lagoon. They exhaled 15-foot high columns of mist into the morning air. The ocean water cascaded off their bodies to create a glistening white "aura" silhouetting their gray bodies. I grabbed my camera for a dozen shots of the miracle below me. They played in the lagoon for 10-minutes before heading north toward their Arctic feeding grounds in Alaska.

(A 36-ton Gray whale and her baby calf popped up right underneath
us at a vista point lookout. They played in the waters below us for
10 minutes before steaming north to Alaska waters to feed.)

"Man," I muttered to myself. "Are we the luckiest cyclists on the coast
this morning or what!"

At another point, a line of pelicans glided over the waves as they flew
in formation just for me. Another 50 white seagulls flew one behind the
other in a "flying line of dental floss" for my imagination. Behind them,
a flock of 50 gray birds flew inches above the Pacific waters.

As we stood on the cliff, a 21-year-old girl hopped out of her convertible
Mustang along with a friend.

"What are you doing?" she said, pointing to my sign.

"Riding from Canada to Mexico," I said.

"You're insane," she said, rather judgmentally. "Why not drive a car?"

"Could you please make that, 'Insanely happy!'" I said.

"No, I'll keep with insane," she said.

"Just look down over the cliff to see that gray whale and her calf,"
Sandi said. "You might redefine the word 'insane' in your notebook."

She and her girlfriend looked over the edge to see the mother whale

101

and her calf. The same aura of sparkling bubbles silhouetted their bodies. They exhaled more shafts of mist into the air. You couldn't ask for a more perfect moment with Nature showcasing her finest magic.

"Whatever," the second girl said as they jumped into their car and sped off.

Sandi said, "We may be the last generation to actually appreciate the natural world. We don't have ear buds stuck into our ears all day and we're not addicted to smart phones. If that's old fashioned, let's keep it that way."

"I'm with you, Sandi," I said.

Without a doubt the Big Sur creates "moments" that stay with you for your lifetime. Whether you write them down in your journal or they burn into your legs, you remember all of it.

At the next point, a small crowd watched five dolphins surfing the waves. I stopped to talk with them and share their wonder. It reminded me of a John Muir quote from years ago, "How many hearts with warm red blood in them are beating under the cover of woods and water, and how many teeth and eyes are shining? A multitude of animal people, intimately related to us, but of whose lives we know almost nothing, are as busy about their own affairs as we are about ours." January 1898

(Frosty standing near a cliff on Big Sur.)

That night, we found a campsite to watch a stunning sunset over the waves.

Next morning, we rode through more and more of the same for 75 miles. We stopped for lunch at Lucia Restaurant overlooking the ocean. Wow! Later toward evening, we stopped at Gorda at the end of the Big Sur. We met Woogi Shen, a Korean cyclist riding around the world. Flawless English. We bonded immediately. Just a fine young man exploring the world!

A Spaniard named Juan and his wife bought us some milk shakes. People love to talk to long distance touring cyclists. That evening, we stopped at San Simeon, home of the Hearst Castle. We expected to head up there in the morning.

(Three men watching the sun go down on the Pacific
Ocean. Sublime moment of the ride.)

Chapter 18

HEARST CASTLE

Chapter 18: Hearst Castle, Cambria, fabled coast road

"Dreamers! They built the Wall of China. They erected the Taj Mahal. Dreamers imagined the steam locomotive. They built the stupendous castles in Europe. Down through time, creative people conceived amazing paintings, sculptures, books and songs. It's recorded that Leonardo da Vinci produced drawings for the first bicycle. Creative people built monuments to history like the Roman Coliseum. In America, Frank Lloyd Wright's architectural genius changed the design of buildings. And, for all of the United States, William Randolph Hearst built America's answer to Versailles in France. The Hearst Castle took 15 years to build. In it, he entertained Mary Pickford, Clark Gable, Carol Lombard, Alfred Hitchcock, presidents, athletes, artists and other movers and shakers from around the world. Nonetheless, we weren't prepared for the sheer elegance and regal opulence enjoyed by this one man with a dream." FHW

After we rode past Gorda, the Big Sur slid downward like a snake slithering toward the ocean. On our left, hills swept upwards to the mountains. On our right, the wide Pacific crashed upon the sandy beaches.

We passed a huge elephant seal colony of 5,000 or more. They swim out to sea hunting for food eight months of the year. Once full and fat, they lounge on the beaches for four months to birth their pups and bark at each other for no apparent reason. Additionally, they use their flippers to toss sand on their bodies while snuggling up against each other for some kind of brotherly love.

(Standing in the garden in front of the Hearst Castle with statues from Roman and Greek times decorating the grounds.)

We camped out near the beach. In the morning, we bought tickets at the base of the mountain. A bus carried us to the castle.

At the top around 1,000 feet, the bus let us off at the base of 85 steps to the main portion of the castle. Surrounding us, elegant marble statues, flowerbeds and white globe-lights sat atop stylish poles. At the top of the stairs, where some of the most famous Hollywood stars of all time once walked, the front of the castle featured flowered pools filled with fish, walkways to the edge where you could look out to the ocean and more white marble statues from Roman and Greek history.

A guide named Gary Lundquist picked us up for a walk into the "Great Rooms" of the castle. We passed through elegant doors to find ourselves standing in a massive drawing room with paintings, woven wall-hangings and accented furniture.

Lundquist said, "You are standing in one of 165 rooms meant to spellbind each visitor. You walked through the same door as Humphrey Bogart, Babe Ruth, Grace Kelly, Kathryn Hepburn, James Stewart, Liz Taylor and other sports and screen stars.

"Hearst built an airport to fly people into his castle for legendary parties featuring his large indoor and outdoor pools. His dining room featured a 100-foot long table. He ordered 100 different ceilings for the various rooms in his castle."

From what I understood, Hearst's castle would cost $400 million in today's money. Additionally, he owned the largest zoo in America at the time of his financial power. He let no whim or fantasy escape him. With his vast sum of inherited and publishing money, he created anything and everything he wanted.

He constructed tennis courts, indoor and outdoor swimming pools, hot tubs, steam rooms, pool rooms, skeet ranges, a large zoo, horse stables, croquet lawns, bathrooms to serve every bedroom, library and lounges. He developed a movie theater still in operation today.

Striding into the indoor pool, you walk on gold inlayed tiles. White marble statues surround the crystal-clear pool.

Two towers soar over the entire castle and can be seen for miles along the California coast.

Hearst, 1863-1951, a publisher and journalist, owned 18 newspapers and 9 magazines including Good Housekeeping and Harper's Bazaar. As stated thus far, he lived a flamboyant life filled with love affairs and sensational journalism. Beyond that, he's credited with helping sway public opinion toward the Spanish-American War.

His father struck upon riches as a silver miner in the 1850's. When William reached the age of ten, his mother took him on a journey through Europe. He became enthralled with castles of the Old Country. He vowed as a child to one-day build a castle greater than any in Europe. By 1915, he inherited his father's wealth in gold and turned it into diamonds with his publishing and movie making empire. He fathered five children, but he lived at the castle while his wife ran her own life in New York City. Ultimately, he owned six castles in the USA and Europe.

Today, the castle stands as a monument to opulence, history, art and ideas. He loved the arts, which may be seen all over the castle, including Roman art from 2,000 years ago. He loved parties and dancing. He loved horses. He loved sports. All in all, he lived a wild and satisfying life to die with a smile on his face at 88 years of age.

(Endless steps lead to statues, gardens, fountains and
views of the Pacific Ocean at the Hearst Castle.)

As we walked around the castle, we couldn't help but think that the money he spent on such a monument heralded back to the egos and power of King Louis the 14th of France at Versailles. Today, we see Bill Gates in his mega-mansion replete with lake, tennis courts and servant staff. Donald Trump builds entire hotels in his own name: Trump Tower. One look along the California coastline near Los Angeles offers $10 million mansions by the boatload. Scanning the yachts in San Diego harbor makes you wonder how anyone could amass such money.

If you look back in time, every king built something like the pyramids, Ming Dynasty Tombs, Disneyland and Machu Pichu in honor of his ego. In the end, the great leveler: old age and death.

At the end of a fascinating day at the castle, we boarded the bus for a ride back to the parking lot. Hundreds of people milled around the visitor center. Some of Hearst's kids still thrive as they own huge entertainment industries. His famous grand-daughter, Patty Hearst, once kidnapped and forced into becoming a terrorist, spent time in jail, but today runs some of the Hearst Empire.

(Indoor pool with gold inlay tiles everywhere you walk. Spas, steam rooms, bubbling hot tubs and marble statues.)

After such an eye-opener, we felt happy to be healthy and free enough to live our lives in a good home with food to eat and friends for fellowship. We especially enjoyed our passion for bicycle travel all over the planet. All in all, William Randolph Hearst lived a great life and we are still living our marvelous lives.

We jumped on our bikes for a ride to the San Simeon State Park and a hot meal with several other cyclists riding down the West Coast. We sat by the campfire that night swapping stories.

As I sat back looking at the dying embers of the fire, I said with a grin, "You know something…it doesn't get any better than this."

Sandi said, "You are so right, dear."

Chapter 19

CALIFORNIA BEACHES

Chapter 19: Endless California beaches, people, volleyball, surfers, Santa Monica Pier, end of Route 66

"After an epic moment on your bicycle during a long-distance tour, whether it manifests as two condors gliding down to check you out on the El Camino Highway in Bolivia at 15,000 feet, or riding your bicycle when a family of penguins waddles up to you in Antarctica, or you meet with an emu named George in the Australian Outback, or you strike up a conversation with a man walking across America on his hands—and a hundred other magical moments—you don't want that 'moment' to end. You want to experience it for as long as possible. After riding Big Sur, we didn't want those two days to terminate. But, as we stopped at Gorda, California, the finality of Big Sur landed on us. We knew our 'moment' with that wondrous ride had reached its conclusion. Yet, we knew that by continuing to pedal our bicycles, we anticipated yet another 'moment' because life always moves forward. Movement constitutes the lifeblood of bicycling. Life moves with you and opens to you on an adventure. Pedal into it, live it, love it and thank your lucky stars that you ride your two-wheeled iron steed into that sheer magic." FHW

We noticed one thing that occurred when we camped out at the San Simeon State Park north of Cambria. The park personnel placed Porta-potties in front of the locked bathrooms due to the lack of water. Additionally, at a restaurant in the morning, they didn't serve water unless asked. Along the route, brown grass dominated the landscape. The Los Angeles Times reported that 12 million trees died in 2018 from lack of rainfall. They said, "California faces an 'exceptional drought' with no end in sight."

After pedaling to Morrow Bay, we witnessed 10,000 seabirds circling a chunk of the ocean about the size of four football fields pieced together. They flew in such a manner as to resemble a tornado splashing down on the ocean.

"My God," I gasped. "That's incredible!"
"Takes your breath away," said Sandi.
"What causes such a gathering?" I asked.
"Mostly food," Sandi said.

(Kite-surfers along the West Coast. They rip past the waves out toward the open sea, only to turn around and ride more waves back into the beaches while flying into the air with the aid of the wind.)

We continued toward Arroyo Grande where we met an old cycling friend Jim Twentyman and his friend Susan Ratalo, a fabulous Italian chef. We shared an evening of food, wine and warm conversation. It's amazing that each of us carries the stories of our lives around us like a suitcase only known to ourselves. At any given moment, we blurt out our joys, sorrows, frustrations and political persuasions.

From Arroyo Grande, we pedaled through unending fields of strawberries, celery and cabbage. Many of the crops grew right up to the ocean cliffs. We watched many field-hands working their fingers to the bone as they installed irrigation systems, picked fruit and crated farm goods. Talk about hard work with no let-up! I remember my youth picking cucumbers for two cents a bushel. I cut, baled and mowed hay from dawn to dusk. One thing hit me: your birth lotto number could easily be either fortunate or unfortunate depending on your parents and the location of your birth.

(Fun way to make a living on the beaches of California. Yes,
he landed on his feet to the roar of the crowd.)

While we have pedaled through third world countries, we thanked our lucky stars we weren't born into such unending poverty with no hope of climbing out of it. Fate plays a huge part in your life.

By the time we reached the beautiful city of Santa Barbara, we wore ourselves out climbing and descending 2,200-foot mountain passes as well as riding through a lot of dry, hot desert. We carried two gallons of water at all times. For all of California's beauty, it features some pretty arid territory.

At Santa Barbara, we noticed Lamborghini's, Ferrari's, Bentley's and Rolls Royce's. More than a few folks enjoyed huge bank accounts in that neck of the woods.

"Sandi," I said. "Do you notice a lot of expensive sports cars flying by us?"

"Maybe you could buy me one for my birthday," she said.

"Sure, I'll whip out my credit card for $450,000.00," I said.

We pitched our tent 12 miles south of Santa Barbara at Carpinteria State Park. They charged $10.00 per night instead of the usual $5.00 at the "Hiker-Biker" site.

"Why double the camping charge?" I asked.

"It discourages the homeless from trashing the place," said the ranger.

"Why penalize the rest of us?" I asked.

"No other way to stop them because they have equal rights to camp here," she said. "But they stink of alcohol and drugs, and they trash the place every time."

"Great," I said.

In the campground, we met German riders, Swiss, Canadian and Dutch. Additionally, we met 39-year-old 6'7", lean, handsome, college graduate Travis who yearned to make the pro volleyball circuit, but instead got drunk too much and lost his youth. He didn't know what to do with himself. We hopped into our tent, but he slept in the grass to avoid the camping fee.

We woke up early and packed. As we stepped onto our pedals to head south, Travis staggered out of the brush to ask me if he could go with us.

"You look like hell," I said. "Are you okay?"

"I got drunk last night," he said. "Can I ride with you two today?"

"Listen, we're going to hammer a lot of miles today and you're not in any shape to stay with us."

"I guess you're right," he said.

"Take care of yourself," I said. "Please find a job, purpose and passion for your life. It's a lot easier to wake up to a positive day instead of recovering from being drunk."

We blew by Huntington, Pismo, Malibu and more beaches. Each featured volleyball nets, bikini-clad women, dogs, beach balls, surfers and silly looking people.

At one beach, colorful kite-board-surfers harnessed the wind to ride out on their surfboards while they leapt over incoming waves and upon their return, screamed back over them inbound. Their sails colored the sky. As a windsurfing veteran myself, I knew they enjoyed one heck of a wild and crazy time out on the ocean.

(With gas prices hitting $5.00 a gallon in California,
this sign might become the future.)

In Los Angeles, we pedaled through Venice Beach with all its variety and Muscle Beach with all its Arnold wannabee's. Thousands flocked to the beaches and thousands more sold trinkets, presented acrobatic shows and, the religious folks tried to persuade everyone that "sin" didn't pay.

No question, southern California fits the Beach Boys' classic songs like, "I got a '34 wagon and I call it a woody…surf city, here we come… it's not very cherry, it's an oldie but a goodie…."

One of the things you notice along the beaches of Los Angeles: great disparity of rich and poor folks. Big money and no money. Good life and life on the streets. Some enjoy boundless wealth while others live on handouts and homeless shelters.

After watching a particularly excellent acrobatic show, we pitched a buck into the bucket before pedaling south toward San Diego.

Chapter 20

MAKING THE MEXICO BORDER

Chapter 20: Making the Mexican border

"*No matter how long your bicycle tour, no matter how many miles, no matter how many campfires and no matter how many amazing moments you experienced—your journey ultimately comes to an end. It might be a coast-to-coast, border-to-border or continent-to-continent, but like Thomas Stevens' first bicycle journey around the world 1884 to 1886—you ultimately come to the finality of your expedition. Captain Jean Luc Picard of the Starship Enterprise said it best, 'Someone once said that 'time' is a predator that stalks us all our lives. I rather believe that 'time' is a companion that goes with us on a journey. It reminds us to cherish each moment, because it will never come again. What we leave behind is not as important as how we lived.' Relish the highs, endure the lows and savor the in-between times. Remember the good, bad and ugly times. Stand tall that you possessed the courage to explore the world on your iron steed. It provided you wings to fly. It carried you to your dreams and you pedaled it into yet another adventure.*" FWH

After wandering through the endless street vendors, we pushed our bikes further down the coast until we arrived at Sonoma Beach, north of San Diego.

This story may delight and intrigue you because it couldn't have occurred without the Internet. It's about a boy who meets a girl. Boy takes girl out to the high school prom from the cross-town rival. Boy dances with girl. Boy kisses girl on front porch. The boy says, 'good night'. Boy never sees girl for the rest of his life, or, should I say, 'most of the rest of his life'.

About five years ago, after writing one of my commentaries that published nationally, I received an email from the 'girl' that I took to the high school prom in Albany, Georgia over 50 years ago. Judy enjoyed basketball star status at her high school. She asked me to her prom at Albany High School. After that night, I never saw the high school beauty again.

(Sandi riding along the eternal waves of the Pacific Ocean.)

But, because of the Internet, she read one of my columns on environment here in the USA. She obtained my email address. She not only sent me an email, but an attachment of a picture of our prom night together.

She wore a lovely floor-length gown. I pinned a corsage to her dress. I stood like a deer in the headlights with a white sport coat and pink carnation! Just like the famous song still played today!

"I'll be darned," I said.

"Hope you like the picture," she wrote in the email.

We kept contact annually with Christmas cards. On this ride along Route 101, Sandi and I passed right beneath her office window in Sonoma Beach. I called her up to make a date for lunch.

She became a CPA to TV and movie stars along with sports stars. We knocked on her office door. The receptionist welcomed us into a very chic waiting room. Within five minutes, Judy, Sandi and I were seated at a restaurant down the street sharing our lives. She still maintained her statuesque frame and elegant style. She raised a family and stayed married to her fantastic husband, Chris, of 50 years.

Having seen her for the last time that one night in high school, and now, 50 years later seeing her a lifetime ago, well, it pretty much blew my mind. We laughed. We shared. We remembered. After two hours, her office called about an appointment she needed to keep. We bid adieu. I kissed her on the cheek and gave her a big hug. Sandi gave her a big hug, too.

"Wow," I said. "This has been a treat. Thank you and many blessings on your next 50 years."

"Ya'll come back to see us, ya' hear," she said.

And with that, she vanished out the door. We finished lunch before mounting our bicycles for the ride south. Talk about how fast time flies! Try not seeing someone for 50 years and then, suddenly, you come face to face with that person! She experienced her unique life and I lived a whole different life. Now, both of us stand at the end of our lives. Pretty heady stuff!

We pedaled through San Diego for a stop at the aircraft carrier "Midway" that saw a lot of action in the South Pacific in WWII. Near the carrier, WWII submarines floated at the dock with tours to experience how it felt to be a submariner. On a spit of land near the aircraft carrier, we noticed the iconic photograph of a sailor grabbing a nurse on the streets of New York City and kissing her. Someone turned the picture into a 50-foot statue. You could tell the sheer joy of the war being over and peace breaking out all over America.

"Let's duplicate the same kiss," I said to Sandi.

"Okay, you big handsome devil," she said.

We put the camera on 10-second delay and recreated that iconic kiss as a couple of cyclists.

Another twenty miles of traffic found us face to face with the Mexican border. It's a funny feeling to finish an epic journey. We are appreciative for our safety and that no one ran over us. We are thankful for the grit and gumption it takes to pedal through rain, heat and mountains. The West Coast proved itself dramatic, dynamic and extraordinarily beautiful on many levels.

(Frosty standing near the Mexico border sign at the end of our trip.)

What do we remember most? Gees, all of it! But if you pinned us down, that night with the three guys sitting on a rock on the beach watching the sun go down takes the cake for a sublime moment. Additionally, that

36-ton mama whale with her calf surfacing and blowing their snouts right below us, lingers with us for a lifetime. Sandi and I slept in the redwoods and held hands on the beaches. I am thankful for Sandi sharing the ride with me. And to each kind person who shared a moment with us or a conversation or a friendly wave, "thank you" in return and pass it forward.

This is a note from Sandi: to every woman who married a man who likes to wander, hang on tight for some amazing experiences all over the planet. I feel fortunate enough to have worked my whole life, brought up two great kids and now, with retirement, I get to travel to exotic places. I am so excited about bicycling the 'boot' of Italy to see Rome, Venice, Pisa, Florence and Naples. I want to cycle through Greece all the way to the Parthenon in Athens. Then, off to New Zealand for three months of riding. For any ladies who want to take a marvelous ride, try the Lewis & Clark Trail from Astoria, Oregon to St. Louis, Missouri. Oh, and another thing, try those bicycle-barge trips in Europe. Totally fabulous! Eat, pedal, sleep and be happy.

Upon touching the border, we stood astride our trusty iron steeds, Condor and Gracie, for yet another grand journey. "Thank you, old friends," we said. "Thanks for the safe journey."

In the end, we are thankful to all who came before us. We especially like what the Roman philosopher Epictetus said, "Tentative efforts lead to tentative outcomes. Therefore, give yourself fully to your endeavors. Decide to construct your character through excellent actions. And determine to pay the price for a worthy goal. The trials you encounter will introduce you to your strengths. Remain steadfast; for one day you will build something that endures; something worthy of your potential."

I turned to Sandi to give her a lingering kiss.

"Well," she said. "That's a lovely finish!"

Chapter 21

YOU WANT TO BICYCLE ACROSS AMERICA OR THE PLANET?

"Are you over 60 or 70? Do you want to sit on your derriere for the rest of your life without experiencing something epic you wanted to accomplish? What's in a lifespan? What's in retirement? What's it like to get your face into the wind? Old age can either kill you with idleness or it can energize you with curiosity, passion and purpose. Bicycle touring renders all three, big time!" FHW

WHAT IS IT LIKE BEING A LONG-DISTANCE BICYCLE RIDER?

"Why are you riding your bicycle across America, sir?" asked a twenty-something.

"It's a long story, son," I replied.

What is it like being a long-distance touring rider? Is it exciting? Does it make traveling special? What makes me do it? How is it traveling on a bicycle? I am asked these questions often while I'm on tour and I try to explain it to folks.

On an emotional level, it's a sensory involvement with natural forces surrounding me. It's a tasting of the wind, a feeling of the coolness, and the warmth—swirling clouds above me and grasses bending in soft breezes. Touring puts me into intimate contact with sunrises and sunsets.

Along seacoasts, I watch waves charge their white fury against sandy beaches. Touring, in its elegant silence, allows me to see an eagle swoop out of the blue, and with its talons extended, grab a mouse and lift into the sky headed toward its nest. Touring allows me to see a kangaroo hop across the road in Australia or ride into the teeth of an approaching storm.

I witness quiet and wild moments depending on nature. When I am a long-distance touring rider, I get caught up in the forces that swirl around me, and I feel at peace with them. The wild everyday occurrences on the road, which seem extraordinary to many people, are normal to me. Why? Because I place myself in a wilderness 'orbit' that synchronizes with the natural and the animal world—far away from the maddening din of humanity's cities.

My journey carries me through deserts, mountains, forests and plains. As I ride along, three aspects of living become important with every turn of the pedals. Whether I ride through a country or across a continent, I meet people and see the sights. For me, the most important aspect is my connectedness, a combination of what I feel is important in keeping my life in relationship with the natural world, and therefore, myself—and that is—keeping my body, mind and spirit in balance.

I feel that life provides a moving drama that I enjoy exploring. A friend of mine, Duncan Littlefair said that when you walk forward, it's not that you walk forward, you fall forward, you're falling forward into the unknown, and the only thing that prevents you from falling down face first is that you put your other foot out and stop your fall, yet you continue falling into the unknown with each step.

I think bicycling replicates that metaphor. I ride into each day having no idea what's going to happen. I ride with a positive attitude, and invariably, good things happen. It's rare that I ever ride into a negative situation—because life proves generally positive. Some people may complain that it's raining out today, so that's a negative. I don't see it that way. Rain makes flowers bloom. A mountain rises ahead. I have to drop into granny gear. It's a lot like anyone's life as they grow toward their own fulfillment. Each day, I feel as I ride my bike into the unknown, the pedals move around in a constant rhythm of adaptation to the different kinds of terrain, and so do I, with my body, mind and spirit.

Starting with the body, a long-distance touring rider concerns himself or herself with health. That concern translates into taking care of it. I exercise all the muscles, not just the ones for riding a bike because it's important to keep everything balanced.

My nutritional approach is vegetarian with an emphasis on raw natural foods—vegetables, fruits, nuts, grains. I compliment them with whole breads and pastas. I avoid meats and dairy products. This nutritional stance gives my body maximum clean burning fuel to push the pedals throughout the day. It makes me capable of responding to any physical needs whether it be hot, dry deserts such as the Atacama of Chile, the Outback of Australia, or a 15,000-foot pass in the Bolivian Andes. I can move through them with confidence because my body maintains a balance.

The five bodily senses play an important part of the day on a bicycle tour. I feel everything around me. I taste, touch, hear, smell and see nature. I taste the rain on my tongue and touch the bark on a tree. I hear an owl hooting and smell a skunk. I see colors of the rainbow or a stunning sunset. My senses soar because I am involved with the swirling forces of nature. I sweat in the desert and get chilled in the mountains. I am wild on my bicycle with the wind blowing past me.

Touring fills my mind with expectation. Something new lies around the next bend in the road ahead. It can be confusing or frustrating. Most of the time, however, it's a positive experience. If you pinned me down, I would go with the word—serene. Nature creates inexplicable beauty. I love seeing her creativity for the first time and my mind swallows it in big gulps.

Ultimately, my spiritual being moves through the natural world. I pedal, change gears, drink water, see an eagle, watch a storm, and sleep beneath the stars. These activities affect something deep down in my spirit. It's the balance in my life. It's something I can't really know, yet it seems to grow as I grow older. It's a feeling inside me about life, which leaves me at peace with myself.

Chapter 22

EPIC MOMENTS ON TOUR

"Epic moments occur on every bicycle journey. They might be called 'stunning moments' or 'astounding moments' or just plain 'wild and crazy' moments that pop up out of nowhere at any time or any place. There's no way to anticipate them or wish for them. They just flat-out happen to you while you're on a bicycle tour. On this West Coast ride, the mama whale with her calf moment, the Elephant seals moment, Hearst Castle moment, meeting my high school prom date moment and many other subtle 'moments' brought great joy to Sandi and me. For a special treat, I want to share with you a number of spectacular moments during some of my other rides around the world. They may delight you as much as they fascinated yours truly." FHW

TALONS FROM THE SKY: COILED SCALES ON THE GROUND

Heading eastbound across southern California, the sun set low in the sky. Sandi and I looked for a campsite in the rocky terrain east of Joshua Tree National Monument.

"We better find a spot soon," Sandi said.

"I'm looking," I said.

Up ahead, we noticed a fluttering hawk, holding its position as the sky effervesced into pink-white thunderheads in the twilight. Very still! Very quiet!

We pedaled the bikes toward the hawk on that lonely highway. The bird continued its fluttering like a helicopter holding position in order to land. We pedaled closer, closer—until we rode up to the perfect camp spot 100 feet off the highway behind some big rocks.

"I'm going to check out that hawk," I told Sandi.

"I'll get the tent set up," she said. "You want pasta for dinner?"

"Sounds great," I said. "I've got Pesto in my pack."

Quietly excited, I crept over several 20-ton rocks on my way to get under the hawk. He kept flutter until, suddenly, he dove straight down.

I hurried over rocks and dirt until I crept up to where I figured he landed. Before me, not 20 feet away, in a dirt arena surrounded by rocks, the hawk stood in front of a transfixed rattlesnake. The big bird hopped into the air as it dared the rattler to strike. And yes, the rattler complied by lunging at the hawk. Quickly, the snake recoiled into striking position.

The hawk, using his wings and talons, jumped back into the sky toward the head of the snake, toying with him, and daring him to strike. The rattler struck again, but the hawk danced out of the way. For the next 10 minutes the hawk danced into the air toward the rattler, but avoided the snake's deadly fangs.

They pirouetted the dance of life and death. One looked for dinner while the other struggled for life. One dared death while the other lunged for its life.

I crouched in the rocks transfixed with wonder. Sometimes, I cannot help but thank the bicycle gods for their gifts to me as I travel around this planet on Condor, my iron steed. Who could serve up a moment like this? Who could dream it? Who could imagine it? I have witnessed dozens of moments like this one. Each time, I feel tremendous gratitude for this sublime journey on a bicycle.

Before me, the snake struck, and then recoiled. The hawk hopped up to dare the reptile to strike, again and again. Each time, the snake grew wearier and more fatigued. Until, as the last rays of the sun slipped below the horizon, the snake made one last strike for its life, but the hawk seized it by the head with his talons. Seconds later, he pecked it on the head until it died in his clutches.

Moments later, the great hawk flapped his mighty wings with the snake securely gripped in his talons. The elegant bird took to the sky with dinner for his family. One life lost to give life to another. I watched the mighty hawk fly into the sunset for a memory that sticks with me through the years.

This enchanting moment visits me often when I move into Nature. Without a doubt, Condor carries me into exquisite life-moments that render poetic beauty, life and death struggles, mountain heroics and storms that fulfill my spirit.

Such moments cause me to write this about the Power of Adventure:

"When coyotes howl outside your tent, that may be adventure. While you're sweating like a horse in a climb over a 12,000-foot pass, that's adventure. When howling headwinds press your lips against your teeth, you face a mighty adventure. While pushing through a raging rainstorm, adventure drenches you. But that's not what makes an adventure. It is your willingness to struggle through it, to present yourself at the doorstep of Nature. Can any greater joy come from life than living inside the 'moment' of an adventure? It may be a fleeting 'high', a stranger that changes your life, an animal that delights you or frightens you, a struggle where you triumphed, or even failed, yet you braved the challenge. Those moments present you uncommon experiences that give your life eternal expectation. That's adventure!"

I'M HAPPY BEING UGLY

"Climb the mountains and get their good tidings. Nature's peace will flow into you as sunshine flows into trees. The winds will blow their own freshness into you, and the storms their energy, while cares drop off like autumn leaves." John Muir

Heading toward Glacier National Park in Montana, I camped out at Flathead Lake on Route 93 the night before I pedaled into Kalispell.

It felt cool sleeping in late July. The day warmed up as I headed into the gateway to Glacier. I spent an hour in town picking up a new tube and chain oil. The past two weeks presented me with terrible flat tire luck. Every "goat-head thorn" in Montana decided to claim my rear tire as the perfect resting-place for its sharp personality. My spare tube suffered so many patches it resembled the suction cups on an octopus' tentacles.

After loading up on bananas and a watermelon, I readied myself for the 35-mile climb into Glacier Park. Before getting started, I gobbled four bananas. That made me hungry for a small watermelon I had purchased at a grocery, so I cut it into sections and ate them. People walking past laughed as I hung the banana skins on top of my rear pack under a bungee cord. It looked like a fresh kill of bananas.

One couple with their teenage daughter asked a lot of questions as to how much I ate. I told them on a 100-mile day on the flats, I burned between 7,000 to 8,000 calories. But my average daily distance proved more like 60 to 70 miles. In the mountains, I average 50 miles per day, but still burn a lot of calories because of the foot-pounds exerted in the climbs.

The highest mountain pass I ever climbed: in Bolivia at 15,500 feet on a gravel road. That burned a lot of calories in the thin air. But the craziest day of my life: friends talked me into an insane 200-mile day in New Mexico and Texas. My friends and I calculated that we each burned a total of 15,500 calories in 17.5 hours of riding.

While I talked, the girl's spirit brightened, and I saw a sparkle in her eyes. I may have inspired her to try world bicycle touring. As they walked away, she tugged on her mom for permission to go on a tour someday. I heard the mother reply, "That's for people with wanderlust, not you dear."

I wanted to catch them and correct the parent by telling her that I had met dozens of women bicycle touring in countries around the world. I wanted to say that everyone has that "wanderlust" and all they have to do is act on their dreams before they are convinced by their friends or parents to do what's "normal." What's normal usually means settling down and getting a job. My father said, "Do it while you're young, because once you settle down, you've got to take care of responsibilities."

My smart dad! I wish everyone could reserve their early 20's for world travel, to give them greater perspective about people and conditions around the globe. They would come home richer in spirit and understanding.

They would enjoy a greater environmental appreciation for our fragile planet. Furthermore, anyone can ride a bicycle around the world if they choose to do it. However, long ago, I decided to keep quiet and let people make their own choices. I send a secret wish for that girl: "Follow your curiosities; find your dream, chase your dream, catch your dream and live your dream."

After gorging myself on the watermelon, I looked three months pregnant. I waddled over to my bicycle. Moments later, sweat poured from me as I climbed a hill out of town. I might make Glacier by nightfall.

Up ahead, right in the middle of a side road, I saw a man waving his cowboy hat at cars. As I drew closer, a red plaid shirt covered his thin features along with worn jeans, and pointed boots topped off with a ten-gallon, black Stetson.

"You," he yelled, waving his hat at me. "Come over here!"

"What's the problem?" I asked, not wanting to be hassled.

"Why in tarnation ain't you ridin' a horse, or drivin' a pickup, or anything besides that thar' bicycle?" he drawled, drunk as a skunk.

"I like to go slow and I don't have to feed my bike or put gas into it," I said, stopping in front of him.

"Well I'll be damned," he said, scratching his scruffy black beard, peppered with gray. "Ain't nothin' like it used to be. Well, I'll tell you what young fella'. I'm gonna' buy you a drink."

"I don't drink, sir."

"You don't drink?"

"Nope!"

"Well, sir, would you set down at that bar over yonder and tell the Ugliest Man in Montana why you ride a bicycle instead of a horse?

"Who is the ugliest man in Montana?"

"You're lookin' at 'em and I'll prove it."

Even while drunk, he seemed interesting enough, so I walked my bike over to the bar he mentioned. We walked into a log cabin that featured stuffed animal heads on the walls, including grizzly bears, elk, moose, badgers, trout and geese. Traps, guns, bows and arrows rounded out the artillery that decorated the back of the bar. I wanted to sit down in one of the wooden booths, but he pulled me to the bar. I quickly understood why. Up over the cash register hung a large picture of a man with a rifle walking out of the woods dragging a bear. It was titled: "The Ugliest Man in Montana." It looked exactly like my newfound friend.

"That's you isn't it?"

He cocked his head as he rubbed the hairs growing off the top of his nose, "Shore 'nuff, it's me, that bear was one of the toughest fights of my life."

"You fought a grizzly?"

"It weren't but a few years back when I had to battle the meanest and hungriest bear in Montana. He was so big, that my ole friend Paul Bunyan wouldn't come to help me."

"No kidding," I said, realizing that I was about to hear a story.

"Yep," he said. "I was cuttin' timber one day, usin' a ten-pound ax, when this varmint comes into our camp and headed for the cook's tent. Well sir, them lumberjacks scattered for fear of their mangy lives. Not me 'cuz that bear made me mad......by the way, do you want to buy me a beer? My mouth is awful dry."

"Bartender, give us a beer and a sarsaparilla," I said, ready to pay five bucks to hear this man's story. Strangely, he appealed to me. Even in his drunken state, he showed spunk.

"As I was sayin', that bear had me upset because he ate my chicken and dumplins which didn't bother me none, but then that critter gulped down my blueberry pie. Now that got me all fired mad. Nobody eats my blueberry pie and gits away with it."

"Can't blame you," I said, chuckling to myself as this old coot relived his story by swinging his arms and raising the beer to his lips for a swallow.

"There he was slurppin' down my pie when I charged into camp. Soon as he saw me, he knowed he was in trouble 'cuz he ceased slurppin'."

"What'd you do?"

"Why, I done what any self-respectin' lumberjack woulda' done," he said, sweeping the hair out of his face. "I ran over ta' where he was standin' and grabbed a-hold of his tail and bounced 'em betweenst a couple of trees. I thrashed 'em and I bashed 'em and then I thrashed 'em some more."

"What was the bear doing during this bashing?" I asked.

"Whall, he was so ah' scared for his life that he crawled out of his fur and ran off into the woods and nobody done ever heard of him agin'."

"You must have been a bit sore after the fight weren't you?"

"Whall now, I had a few calluses on my hands, but nuthin' to speak of....o' course, there was another time when I was face to face with this killer...."

"That's okay, Ugly," I said, seeing his empty beer glass, which meant the next round was coming out of my pocket. "I've got to be getting down the road."

"I guess yore right sonny."

"By the way, what's your real name?"

"You can call me, Ugly," he said. "It don't matter what you do in this life, as long as you're happy. I'm happy bein' Ugly."

A mile out of town, I still chuckled to myself over Ugly. I never could understand what makes an alcoholic, but in this case, he had brightened my day with his bravado. In my travels, I've seen rich people, poor people, regular people—and what Ugly said is true—the bottom line in life is being happy.

It's more important than anything else.

SAVAGE MOMENT FOR LIFE AND DEATH IN YELLOWSTONE NATIONAL PARK

On my solo journey from Mexico to Canada on the Continental Divide, I hooked up with two Irishmen for a week, but they cut west after viewing Old Faithful.

When Gerry and Dave pedaled westward, I felt my heart grow sad. At the gate entrance of Madison Junction campground, I paid my bill for the "Hike-biker" section. No laughter that night around the campfire. I pitched my tent in silence. I aired-up my mattress and fluffed up my sleeping bag. I set up my cooking gear and snugged-up my miner's lamp around my head. Darkness crept in silently. I cooked my dinner in silence. I wrote my notes quietly. Loneliness made its way into my soul.

Loneliness is the human condition. Cultivate it. The way it tunnels into you allows your soul room to grow. Never expect to outgrow loneliness. Never hope to find people who will understand you, someone to fill that space. An intelligent, sensitive person is the exception, the very great exception. If you expect to find people who will understand you, you will grow murderous with disappointment. The best you'll ever do is to understand yourself, know what it is that you want, and not let the cattle stand in your way. — Janet Fitch

Thankfully, I like the kind of person I am. I've made my parents proud. As I said at the beginning of this adventure, I broadcast "high vibrational energy" wherever I go. I've heard that, if you radiate friendly vibrations, friends naturally gravitate toward you. If you give love, you will receive love in return. Better to share with Gerry and Dave for a week than not at all. They became another thread in the tapestry of my life. I felt rich, funny and more blessed by having spent such a grand time with two Irishman. I counted my blessings.

Next day, I pulled down my tent and pedaled onto the highway by 6:30 a.m. I rolled along the Gibbon River to pass by a steaming pond on the opposite side of the road. Very quiet. No traffic. I sensed nature's rhythms pulsing through the early morning hour. Soon, I viewed 60 feet of descent and the white water of Gibbon Falls. It resembled a bride's veil. Still no traffic.

Back on the road, I stopped on a bridge with the Gibbon River crossing underneath me. I took a few shots of the rising sun sparkling on the waters. So peaceful.

Once again, I made the adventure my companion. I delighted in sheer beauty all around me. I felt my spirit renewing again at my wondrous journey.

I pedaled with vigor into the clear, crisp morning air, through deep forests and along the Gibbon River about 30 yards away on the west side of the highway. Above the river, a red tail hawk followed the current southward, probably on his breakfast patrol. A big fat buffalo munched grass on the east side of the river. Still no traffic. On my left, on the far side of the river, I noticed a cow elk bending down to take a drink. I love seeing elegant elk, moose and deer. They soothe my soul.

Without warning, I barely caught the big, hairy figure of…oh my God, a grizzly bear…as he crept along the deep grass on the far side of the river until he got within 30 feet of the elk…from out of the grass cover, he charged the elk…she saw him and stood up, startled, and started to bolt backwards away from the river…but within seconds, the 700 pound grizzly ran right into the cow elk and grabbed it by the shoulders with his four inch claws…in a moment, he chewed into the bottom of the elk's neck and twisted his huge anvil head…almost like poetry in motion, his enormous body rode the elk down to the ground…where he held her until she could no longer struggle…she stopped …fell limp…life feeds on life and death feeds life.

"Holy crap," I exclaimed as I stopped Condor in stunned amazement.

While I should have been scared to death, it happened so fast that I just stopped and stared. I stood across the river and 40 yards away from the bear. The grizzly could care less about me. His breakfast laid in a bloody mess in front of him. I ripped out my camera to take pictures. He began feeding on the carcass. He ripped open the belly and chewed on his favorite parts. His bloody muzzle turned bright red.

I stood behind a tree, but still astride Condor just in case I had to ride like the wind. I even pointed Condor downhill to give me more speed, quickly, should the grizzly notice and figure me for dessert. Of course, at 185 pounds, I didn't mean much to his main course of 900 pounds of elk meat.

"My God, am I blessed with this moment," I muttered to myself.

(Grizzly after he killed the cow elk and fed upon it. He took a swim in the river. You can see the red carcass just off to his left.)

Within a half hour, a dozen cars stopped to see why I kept snapping pictures. Soon, a whole slew of cars emptied and folks with 1000 mm lenses snapped pictures off fancy tripods. Shortly, three bald eagles landed by the carcass. The bear walked off a distance and snoozed. The eagles closed in for early morning snacks. Then, Mr. Grizzly woke up in 10 minutes and returned to feeding. Amazingly, he jumped into the river to swat at fish or something. His actions appeared comical from where I stood.

Within the next hour, more tourists arrived. I figured I'd seen the best show of the day and turned Condor northward to seek my fortune around the next bend in the road. I've experienced some amazing moments on Condor, and, this one rides up there with the top 10 of my life. As I said in my quote about bicycle touring, "The long-distance bicyclist carries an insatiable desire to interact with possibilities that may emerge around the next bend in the road. His or her curiosity drives the pedals that turn the wheels. Each cyclist carries a sense of "stubborn joy" into the day. The bicyclist lives in that moment and then pedals forward to the next moment, always advancing, never in retreat."

As John Muir said, "How many hearts with warm red blood in them are beating under cover of the woods, and how many teeth and eyes are shining? A multitude of animal people, intimately related to us, but whose lives we know almost nothing, are as busy about their own affairs as we are about ours."

To that quote, I say, "Holy catfish, what a heck of a start to this day! It doesn't get any better than this."

ARRESTED FOR HAVING TOO MUCH FUN!

"When something becomes too much fun, the government will move swiftly to tax it."

Disgruntled Taxpayer

Outside Vicksburg, Mississippi, on Route 80, my brother Howard and I cranked east through the afternoon heat. Sweat dripped from our noses and splashed onto the top tubes. It ran down our spines in tiny rivulets.

It burned our eyes from beads running down our foreheads. Salt stained our black riding tights like the colors of a Zebra.

Howard and I pedaled through the last month of a coast-to-coast bicycle adventure across America. San Francisco, California to Savannah, Georgia! Our legs glistened with sweat as our muscles labored under the constant downstroke on the pedals.

Up ahead, heat waves rippled off the summer pavement, while a blazing sun baked the weeds along the two-lane highway. Trees lined the road while crows scattered in all directions as we passed. One crow struggled to escape from three sparrows darting in on him. They pecked at his feathers—attempting to drive him away. After each attack, he spun wildly in midair to avoid them.

"Those guys are giving that big fella' a hard time," Howard said, pointing.

"I never have figured out why they attack crows like that," I said, remembering a natural science class from school. "But they could be protecting their nests."

Howard, dripping in a sweat-soaked T-shirt, cranked ahead of me—pulling up his water bottle and spitting as he took the lead. "We should make Vicksburg pretty soon. You want to stop at a salad bar and clean 'em out?"

"Good idea!"

Riding in the South during the heat of the summer months could be compared to pedaling in a steam sauna. Heat cooked us and sweat drenched our clothing.

Howard and I left a trail of droplets from our perspiration-soaked bodies. No matter! We looked forward to seeing the Civil War monuments in Vicksburg. We waved at passing cars. Folks moved at a snail's pace in the Deep South. They defined the term, "laid back."

Southerners got a kick out of our riding cross-country through their towns. They took pictures of us—sometimes having family members gather around our bikes.

We pedaled two fully-loaded mountain expedition bicycles. Condor, my bike, got his name from an experience I had while touring on the El Camino Highway from LaPaz, Bolivia to Arica, Chile in South America. While bumping along on a gravel road with a 2,000 foot drop off to my right, two curious condors swooped down from 18,000 feet while I crossed a 15,500-foot pass in the Andes. Sporting 12-foot wingspans, they glided 20 feet off my handlebars. They eyed me as either a piece of meat or as someone who invaded their airspace. I named my bike "Condor" because I had "flown" with the condors of South America.

On this tour, we enjoyed much attention in Louisiana. Folks snapped pictures of us and wanted to talk a lot. People said the darnedest things about long distance touring riders. They kept us laughing because they thought we were either courageous or crazy.

We talked about the day's 'people adventures' when a black-and-white police cruiser passed us traveling west. We waved at him. He waved back, but did not smile.

I routinely wave to police officers out of respect or fear—I'm not sure which. I know they can give me a ticket for speeding. But, on a bicycle, they can't, so I never give them much thought. I watched him go by in my rearview mirror. A few seconds later, he flipped his car around and turned on his flashing red lights.

"That cop turned around," Howard said, sucking on his water bottle.

"Maybe he got a call for an emergency back down the road," I said, glancing back.

I expected the cruiser to fly past us. But it didn't. The police officer pulled in behind us. I looked in my rear mirror to see him pointing his finger for us to pull to the side.

"That cop is pulling us over," I said.

"Probably for speeding," Howard joked. "Maybe he's going to give us a ticket for going too slow. Now wouldn't that be a good one? No! I've got it! He's going to give us tickets for not having licenses to drive bicycles."

We pulled our bikes to a stop. A rotund, middle-aged officer in a blue uniform got out of his cruiser. He sported a chin like a bullfrog's during mating season. We stood astride our bikes, looking back, not sure why he had stopped us.

"Afternoon boys," he said, walking up to us.

"How are you, sir?" I asked.

"I'm fine," he spoke in a raspy voice. "When I passed you boys, I noticed you were smiling and laughing."

"Yes, sir," Howard said. "We're having a great day. We love it here in

Louisiana. In fact, we're hoping to meet Huckleberry Finn when we cross the Mississippi."

"How far you goin'?" the officer asked, brusquely.

"We're on our way from coast-to-coast," I said. "Pacific to the Atlantic."

"You boys ever had your heads examined for mental righteousness?"

"Beg your pardon?" Howard said.

"You know," he said, "Common sense. Anyone in their right mind wouldn't ride a bicycle across the country."

"Our mom told us we were crazy to ride our bikes across America," Howard said. "But, so far, the craziness hasn't killed us."

The officer looked over our packs as if he might be looking for drugs.

Right then, I didn't like this guy's demeanor. My dad always told us to be polite and keep smiling at a police officer. We should always say "Yes, sir!" or "No, sir!" to a man with a badge. This was one of those times to be extra polite.

"Have you had a good time in Louisiana?" he asked in a stern voice.

"Yes, sir," I said. "We've had a real fine time, and we're looking forward to Mississippi."

"Right now, you're in my jurisdiction," he said. "When I drove by you, it looked like you were having a lot of fun."

"Yes, sir, you could say that," Howard said, with a puzzled look sweeping across his eyes.

"Would you say you're having TOO much fun?" the trooper asked, straight faced.

"TOO much fun?" I said. "Well, er, yes sir, we're probably having too much fun, right, Howard?"

"Yes sir, that's right, we're having too much fun."

The officer stepped closer. He looked serious. Maybe I had seen too many movies depicting stereotypical redneck cops hassling people. Nonetheless, I felt tension in my body. He looked the part—thick neck, crew cut, short fat fingers, belly hanging over his belt, and boots that hadn't been polished in a coon's age.

"I hate to say this boys, but there's an ordinance in this county for havin' too much fun. Because I'm an officer of the law, I'm sworn to uphold that ordinance. I'm gonna' have to write ya'll a citation. May I see some form of identification?"

"Sure, officer," we replied, giving him our driver's licenses.

"A law against having too much fun?" Howard said, with a hint of indignation.

"That's right, boys," he said. "I see you're brothers. You wait here while I write you up."

"Yes, sir," I said.

"I'll be right back in a few minutes," he said, waddling away.

"This is crazy," Howard whispered. "This guy is out to lunch. He's only got one oar in the water. He's 51 cards short of a full deck. This guy's a lighthouse with no light on!"

"Don't say that too loud," I muttered. "He's got a badge and a gun."

"He can't give us a ticket for having too much fun," Howard complained. "That does it! I'm going right into the county courthouse and demand a jury trial on this one. I mean, this is nuts! We can't take this lying down. I'll get the ACLU if I have to. Too much fun, right!"

"I thought he was kidding," I said. "But, he's not kidding."

While we waited, I drank a quart of water and switched my bottles on the down tube to have a full one ready. It was warm water, but quenched my thirst.

Darned if I could figure out what we had done to get this cop upset. But I learned never to argue with a police officer. They commanded absolute authority. Minutes later, he walked up to us with two tickets in hand.

"I know ya'll think this is out of line," he said. "But I don't make the laws…I just enforce them. By the way, I like riding bicycles, too. How come you boys are riding mountain bikes with drop bars?"

"They're more durable, and we don't get many flat tires," I said. "They give a smoother ride. Plus, we have three positions for our hands with drop bars. Straight bars fatigue our hands by keeping them in one position."

"I'll have to remember that," he said. "By the way, I live in Vicksburg. Are you boys hungry?"

"Yes, sir," we replied, not understanding why he was so friendly when he had just given us tickets. "There's a nice restaurant called 'Aunt Dorothy's' with an all-you-can-eat salad bar right after you cross the Mississippi River. You can't miss it," he said, walking back to his car.

He drove toward Vicksburg. I stood there looking at Howard who was just as incredulous as I was.

"What in the devil just happened to us?" I asked.

Howard looked down at his ticket and started laughing.

"What's so funny?" I said.

"Read it," Howard said, chuckling and slapping his thigh.

On the ticket in long hand, it read, "This is a citation to the Wooldridge brothers for having too much fun on their bicycle trip across America. You can either pay a large fine down at the county courthouse, or you can come over to my house (directions below) and take showers plus eat my wife's great cooking. You're welcome to stay overnight. My kids would love to hear about some of your experiences. It would be an honor and a pleasure to have you visit us."

"I'll be hanged," I muttered.

After riding into town that evening, we followed Officer Buford Jackson's directions to his house. We leaned our bikes against the white railing on the front porch of a traditional Southern home where a couple of rockers awaited the evening sunset and friendly conversation.

I knocked. When the door opened, I had never seen a wider smile, a bigger grin, a larger heart, nor a face so full of mirth and mischief as I saw on Buford Jackson at that moment. Behind him, two girls and a boy must have been told that Ricky Martin and Tom Cruise were coming to dinner, because their faces displayed a youthful expectation that something special was about to happen in their lives.

Buford showed us the guest bedroom and hot showers. "Give me all your dirty clothes," he said. "Adeline will have them washed and dried by morning."

"Ask the boys if they like summer squash, green beans and garden tomatoes?" Adeline called from the kitchen.

"We like everything," Howard said.

Buford smiled, "These boys can eat a whole hog and a bucket of mashed potatoes with coleslaw."

"Don't forget the pumpkin pie," Howard said, laughing.

"She just made fresh blueberry pie for tonight," Buford said.

"Break my heart," I said, my mouth already watering at the thought of my favorite pie.

Before we could protest about his washing our clothes, Buford gathered our sweaty shorts, shirts and other dirty clothes and walked off to the laundry room.

That evening, we ate a dinner fit for kings. Adeline Jackson, in a long cotton dress and just a touch of make-up, couldn't have been kinder.

At the table, she sat Howard between the two girls and Zach next to me. I hate to admit this, but my brother is good looking which left the two girls giddy with excitement.

Buford grasped his son's and daughter's hands. Howard and I completed the circle when Buford spoke, "Dear Lord, bless this food...."

After grace, we plowed into the food dishes being passed around the table. Howard struck up the conversation with our starting and finishing point of the ride.

Shirley, nearly 14 with a blond ponytail, asked the first question, "What does San Francisco look like?" Later, Paula, 12 with pigtails, asked, "How many miles do you ride in one day?" Zach, all of eight years old with a crewcut, asked, "Where do you go number '2' if you live in a tent?"

Once they heard about the basics of bicycle adventure, they asked about our favorite moments on the tour. Howard described crossing the Golden Gate Bridge with the sparkling blue waters below and watching the two-masted sailboats plying the waters of the bay. He spoke about our ride into Yosemite where we watched a 'moonbow', a rainbow caused by moonlight, at the base of Bridal Veil Falls. I talked about our ride through Death Valley with 116 degrees heat that felt like riding inside an oven. Later, we pedaled our way to the rim of the Grand Canyon and looked down a mile below to the Colorado River.

Zach's eyes grew wide with wonder as Howard described the Painted Desert and the Petrified Forest. Paula and Shirley could hardly contain themselves before asking the next question.

"You know," Howard said, after answering the last question. "It's not the adventures that count as much as it is the friends we've made along the way. Your daddy and mama are the best story of this trip and you kids are the best, ever! My brother and I are so thankful we ran into your dad."

Howard glanced with a sly smile over at Buford. I added my own "look." We weren't THAT amused when he had given us the tickets for having "too much fun."

Buford shrugged innocently. Then he asked with a grin, "What'd you fellers think after I handed you those tickets?"

"Would 'bewildered' seem to fit?" Howard said. "At first, you were so serious, we didn't know what to think. After you walked back to your cruiser, I was ready to…."

"You don't want to hear Howard's words," I said. "Needless to say, we thought we might be in a Hitchcock movie."

"Just thought I'd put a little humor into your day," Buford said.

"He's a good cop," Adeline said, "but he's a practical joker, too, and he has a heart of gold. We're real glad you boys came over for dinner. Aren't we children?"

At that moment, Shirley, Paula and Zach's faces lit up. They nodded.

"What made you think up giving us tickets?" I asked.

"You know," he said, "it came out of the blue. I guess I wanted my kids to see a bit of the world through some strangers' eyes."

"We have more stories," Howard said.

"They've heard enough. It's time for bed."

"No, daddy, please…." they pleaded.

"You heard me," Buford said.

"This dinner conversation has been great for our kids," Adeline said. "You boys have given them an appreciation for geography, highways, mountains, camping, and most of all, a sense of what's out there."

"Have any of you read 'The Hobbit'?" Howard asked Shirley.

She nodded and said her teacher had read it to the class.

"Well," Howard spoke. "Bilbo Baggins said, 'There's a whole lot of adventure outside your door.'"

"That's right," I said. "It's out there waiting for you when you choose to travel."

Shirley gleamed and followed her siblings to the bathroom to brush her teeth. Who knows what kind of adventure path her life would take? It might be on a bicycle.

The next morning, as we pedaled onto the highway, I was reminded again, as I had been hundreds of times in the past, that people are full of surprises.

In the case of Buford and Adeline, my world became richer thanks to their unexpected hospitality. Shirley, Paula and Zach bring a smile to my heart and mind whenever I think back on that magical evening.

Bless the Jackson's for their love, generosity, sense of humor, and their children with big, bright eyes filled with expectation. I am thankful that most of the world is filled with Buford's and Adeline's, and because it is, we are all blessed with joy at surprising moments in our lives.

In my lifetime, I hope to get arrested many more times for having too much fun.

A BICYCLE MOMENT FROZEN IN TIME

"GREAT GOD, THIS IS AN AWFUL PLACE." ROBERT FALCON SCOTT, 1912

In the morning, a whiteout howled across McMurdo Station, Antarctica with 150-mile-per-hour winds and minus 80-degree temperatures. I had been confined to my barracks for two days as a "Condition One" storm worked its way over the icepack before me.

By late evening, the weather turned placid but a biting minus 40-degree temperature kept most people inside. I, however, bundled into my cold weather gear—insulated boots, heavy mittens, five Thermax layers, fleece, three hats, face protection, along with ski goggles—and headed out the door to ride my bicycle over the ice runway.

Yes, there were bicycles at the scientific station for me to ride. Operations reported some emperor penguins on the ice. I had to see them no matter what the cold. I jumped on my bike looking like an overstuffed bear with all my cold weather gear on. My breath vaporized as I pedaled toward the ice-covered ocean. My lungs burned with each inhalation of polar cold.

About a mile around the cove, the setting sun glinted off the roof of Robert Falcon Scott's Discovery Hut. He had died 90 years ago on his last attempt to reach the South Pole. The hut had stood on the point of McMurdo Sound since 1902. It gave mute testimony to the courage those men displayed in their polar adventures. This was a cold, miserable place.

I rode along a path that led toward the ice pack in the sound. It's hard to describe pack-ice, however, it is a bunch of jumbled, broken ice chards being heaved and smashed into multiple shapes such as triangles, domes, squares, tubulars, and wedges—like an Erector Set gone crazy. However, near the shore, it was reasonably smooth with a thin veneer of snow from the blizzard.

Above me, a gold and purple sky glowed brazenly in its final glory into the crevasses of the Royal Society Range across McMurdo Sound. For once, a rare quiet softened the bitter edge of the crystal white desert before me. One of the glaciers, more than ten miles across at its terminus, radiated liquid gold from the setting sun. Stepping through some shallow snow drifts, I sank knee deep until I pulled through and gained the edge of the ice. Even with polar weather gear protecting my body, the numbing cold crept through the air as if it were trying to find a way into my being.

The bike frame creaked at the cold and the tires made a popping sound on the snow. The big boots I wore made it hard to keep on the pedals. But I persevered and kept moving forward. Across the ice, I looked through the sunlight and saw four black figures approaching. I shaded my eyes with my gloved hand. They drew closer; their bodies were back-lit by the sun on the horizon. It was a family of Emperor penguins. I dismounted from my bike. From our survival classes, I learned to sit down so as not to frighten them. By appearing smaller than them, they might find me interesting.

Slowly, I lowered myself into the snow cross-legged like an Indian chief. Minute by minute, they waddled straight toward me. Three big birds, about 80 pounds each kept moving dead-on in my direction. The smallest followed behind them.

Another minute passed and they were within 30 feet of me. The lead Emperor carried himself like a king. His silky black head-color swept down the back of his body and through his tail. A bright crayon yellow/orange streaked along his beak like a Nike logo. Under his cheek, soft aspirin-white feathers poured downward glistening in lanolin. His wings were black on the outside and mixed with black/white on the front. He stood at least 40 inches tall and his enormous three-toed feet were a gray reptilian roughness with blunted talons sticking out. He rolled his head. He looked at me in a cockeyed fashion, as if I was the strangest creature he had ever seen.

I don't know what made me do it, but I slipped my right hand out of the glove and moved it slowly toward him. The rest of the penguins closed in. The big guy stuck his beak across the palm of my hand and twisted his head, as if to scratch himself against my skin. I felt glossy feathers against my hand. He uttered a muffled "coo." The rest of the penguins cooed. Their mucus membranes slid like liquid soap over their eyes every few seconds. I stared back, wanting to say something to them, but realized I could not speak their language. However, at that moment, we shared a consciousness of living.

My frozen breath vapors hung in the air briefly before descending as crystals toward the ground. I battled to keep from bursting with excitement. Within seconds, one of the other penguins pecked my new friend on the rump. He drew back. With that he turned and waddled away. Following the elders, the little one gave one last look at me, as if he too wanted to scratch my hand, but was afraid, and turned with his friends. As they retreated, their wings flailed outward, away from their bodies like children trying to catch the wind in their arms. The baby Emperor departed as the last to go.

My hand turned numb, so I stuck it back into the glove. As I sat there, I remembered once when a hummingbird landed on my finger in the Rocky Mountains. I remembered the sheer delicacy nature shared with me that warm spring day in the wilderness. Here, in this frozen wasteland beyond the borders of my imagination where man does not belong, nature touched me again today with its pulsing heart and living warmth. I only hope my species learns as much respect for our fellow travelers as they show toward us.

I stood up, tightened my hood and looked for the penguins. They had vanished into the frozen white world in front of me. Only the pack ice rumbled toward the horizon. I turned to my bike. It's hard to believe that two rubber tires laced together with spokes and rims, and attached to a metal frame could carry me from the Amazon Jungle, to Death Valley and on to where the bolt goes into the bottom of the globe.

That simple machine lying in the frozen snow had taken me to far flung places on this planet and it had allowed me magical moments beyond description. That moment with the penguins probably was the best it had ever done by me. I remounted it and turned toward the barracks.

The ride back didn't seem so cold.

WALKING ACROSS AMERICA ON HIS HANDS

"Courage is one thing. A sense of purpose another. When you put them together in one human being, the world can be changed." John Brown

Starting that 1984 summer bicycle tour, I pedaled through heavy traffic for the beginning of my coast-to-coast cycling adventure. The Los Angeles smog choked me for 100 miles into the Mojave Desert. After crossing the Colorado River, I breathed easier when the 'Brown Cloud' flowed south toward Phoenix. I pedaled into cleaner air in the mountains. Climbing steep grades took half the day while coasting down the backside took only 45 minutes.

In New Mexico, I crossed the continental divide and descended into the desert on Route 380. With a blazing sun overhead, I struggled along the two-lane pavement. Sweat dripped from my face and arms. Every breath crowded my mouth with air as dry and hot as cotton balls. Heat waves rippled over the pavement as I descended further into the barren landscape. The thermometer hit 103 degrees by the time I was ten miles out of Roswell, New Mexico.

Ahead, I noticed a lone figure walking along the left side of the road. It was difficult imagining anyone walking down the highway in that torrid temperature.

"I wonder what that guy's doing walking in this heat?" I muttered to myself. "Looks like he's got a dog with him, too."

"That isn't a dog," I gasped seconds later, doubting my eyes, and straining harder to make out what I saw.

It was another man walking on his hands. Within a few seconds, I found out why. His legs were missing!

Less than forty yards away, the lone figure was a man reading a book, walking beside another man walking on his hands. A camper van was parked on the shoulder a half mile ahead. I rode up even with them. Something inside just made me stop and drop my bike in the gravel.

I couldn't help crossing the road, knowing that whomever this man was, he possessed inconceivable courage. What was he doing out here walking on his hands in the desert? He saw me and stopped. He lowered his body down to the ground, resting it on a leather pad that covered his two severed legs just below the groin. His Paul Bunyan upper arms led down to his hands, which grasped two rubber pads. Sweat soaked his T-shirt. His sandy hair framed a tanned, round face punctuated by a pair of clear brown eyes. He flashed a beautiful smile.

"Hi, how ya' doin'?" I said approaching with my hand extended. "My name is Frosty."

"Glad to meet you," he said shaking my hand. "I'm Bob Wieland, and this is my friend, John."

"Pleasure to meet you," I said. "I gotta' tell you Bob, I'm more than a bit curious seeing you out here in the desert."

"The same could be said about you," he said. "What are you doing out here?"

"I'm riding my bicycle across America."

"That makes two of us," Bob added. "I'm walking across. I'd bike but my legs are too short for the pedals."

I laughed. His humor was natural. We bantered a few minutes about the weather. Bob gave me a short history of his journey. He started on the West Coast. He crossed over several 6,000-foot passes. His friend fixed meals, but often, people asked them into their homes for the night. If no one offered a night's lodging, both men slept in the back of the camper pickup. His friend drove the vehicle ahead and came back to walk with him. His companion read a book while guiding Bob down the left side of the highway. Bob lost his legs in combat as a medic in Vietnam. I asked him when he had started.

"I've been out 19 months and have completed 980 miles," he said. "At my speed, I can finish this adventure in three more years, maybe less."

"Why are you doing it?" I asked.

"There's a lot of adventure out here on the road. I suppose I could sit back and get fat watching TV for the next fifty years, but I want to do something with my life. I want to make a difference. I have to make do with what I have left. You know the saying; you only go around once."

"You have my greatest admiration," I said, shaking his hand again.

It was one of those moments where you don't quite know what to do or say. I just met the most incredibly courageous man in my whole life who was looking up at me from the pavement. His legs were gone. He was a man, but he stood only three feet high. His hands had become his feet.

That gray leather pad was belted to his bottom like a baby diaper. Those rubber pads on his hands were his wheel tread on his arduous journey. I gasped inside myself at the enormity of his quest.

"Guess I better get moving," I said, reluctantly.

"Take care," Bob said. "Have a good ride. I'll get there one of these days."

"There's no doubt that you will reach the Atlantic Ocean," I said.

While turning away from that amazing human being, tears filled my eyes. I started crying halfway across the road. What he was attempting staggered my imagination. My friends thought I was nuts taking a transcontinental bicycle trip, but they had no understanding of how easy I had it compared to Bob Wieland. Miles and years down the road—that moment colors my mind as vividly as the day it happened.

Most human beings have handicaps in one way or the other—physical or psychological. What is important is how they handle their limitations. He concentrated on what he could do, not on what he couldn't do. Instead of giving up, Bob pushed forward into the unknown not only determined to succeed, but expecting to succeed.

George Bernard Shaw celebrated people like Wieland when he wrote, "This is the true joy of living, spending your years for a purpose recognized by yourself as a right one...to be used up when they throw you on the scrap heap of life. To have been a force of nature instead of a selfish little clod of ailments and grievances complaining that the world will not devote itself to making you happy."

Bob Wieland pushed himself through 3,300 miles of hardship that few people could comprehend. He gutted his way up mountains, sweated his way across deserts, and fought through raging storms. Every labored breath drew him closer to his goal.

Two years later, I listened to NPR radio while eating breakfast one morning. Bob Wieland reached the Atlantic Ocean thus succeeding in his quest to walk on his hands coast to coast across America.

I sat at the breakfast table crying like a baby because that man had given me courage to face my own struggles from that one meeting in the New Mexico desert. I'm sure he touched thousands more on his remarkable journey across America. Here's to you, Bob Wieland, to your courage, your humor, your passion and your life.

HIGH SPEED CHASE

"I pity the person in a car who drives across the great southwestern desert, and thinks it's boring." Doug Armstrong, 7 continent bicyclist

On Route 72, near Parker, Arizona, I headed east into the twilight. A blistering day scorched my body into a dishrag that had cleaned out a pot of greasy spaghetti and hung over the top tube to dry. My chances of finding a stream for a bath were next to nothing.

Nonetheless, I enjoyed the day. Red flowering cacti filled the air with their sweet scent and pink streaks sliced the heavens into sections while lighting up billowing thunderheads that boiled toward the sunlight. Their tails faded into the eastern darkness. Saucer-like clouds skidded across the sky to the south of me.

Nearing Bouse, I stopped at a closed gas station and parked my bike against the side of the cracked, plaster wall of the building.

"Might as well check the spigot to see if I can get a bath," I said, kneeling by the pumps. "I'll be darned! Water!"

I grabbed my soap, razor and towel. The water shot out of the faucet full blast. I soaked myself down--clothes and all. After soaping up my shirt, shorts and socks, I shaved my face. As usual, my neck resembled a bloody dogfight after the razor finished its business. No matter what the ads say about shavers, they can rip a man's throat to ribbons. Nevertheless, my body tingled at the newfound clean feeling on my skin. After rinsing away the soap from my shorts and shirt, I stepped into clean clothes. I hung my wet tights, socks and jersey onto the back of my pack for quick drying and loaded my water bottles.

Bouse featured ramshackled buildings on flat desert sands. I cranked into the cool evening air. A mile out of town, I scanned the road for a campsite. My tires made the only sound as stillness crept over the land. A few birds flew over the sagebrush and the thunderheads darkened with the fading light.

I don't like being on the road at twilight. Too dangerous!

"Come on, where's a place to camp?" I complained out loud. "I'm out in the middle of nowhere, and can't find a place to sleep."

In the distance, not more than a hundred yards, I saw a building.

"Bingo!" I said. "That looks like home tonight."

In minutes, I would have my tent set up behind the building and be cooking dinner. This highway deserted highway meant a quiet night's sleep.

Just then, a coyote loped along the highway off to my right 30 yards away. He looked intent on something that caught his eye. I pressed harder on the pedals. He continued loping along, not noticing me. He ran ghostlike in the twilight shadows. He moved as quietly as the still air.

As I followed him, he veered toward the high side of the shoulder near a bush. When he approached it, a jackrabbit shot out of the cover, headed straight down the side of the pavement. The coyote changed from loping gear to Warp Factor two. Every muscle in his body coiled. A cloud of dust broke the stillness. The rabbit raced forward with a three step hoppity, hoppity, hoppity hop, then ran four strides like a dog, then three more short half steps, and back to running like a dog. At the same time, the coyote, with his nose cutting into the air like an F-16 jet and his tail streaming behind him, edged closer and closer. About the second the coyote opened his mouth to grab the rabbit, the speedster turned on a dime and shot left across the highway in front of me.

Mr. Coyote pulled his teeth back into his mouth and executed a 90-degree turn. From a dead stop of zero, the coyote accelerated again to high speed. Again, the rabbit raced ten yards along the highway and did another right turn. Mr. Coyote closed quickly.

On the right side of the road again, the rabbit, followed less than a few steps behind by the coyote, leaped across a shallow culvert. Big mistake! As he sailed over the ditch, the dark figure of the coyote leaped faster and higher through the air, like a heat-seeking missile homing in on its prey. In midair, the coyote's teeth reached down and clamped onto the rabbit. When they fell to earth, the rabbit screamed a death cry. Silence!

When I pedaled up to the spot, I saw the coyote, with the rabbit in his mouth, vanish into the darkness.

EVER CHANGE THE OIL IN YOUR KNEES?

"Be like the bird, who when landing on branch too slender, feels it give way beneath him; yet sings, because he has wings. Well, we have wings, wings of the spirit; with this attitude we cannot be defeated. You see, there is a peace of God that goes beyond all our ordinary understanding. I hope you find enough to help you." Victor Hugo, Duncan Littlefair

Heat punctuates the air in South Georgia every summer. Humidity sticks to the skin like plastic sandwich wrap. For riding, the combination is torture. All I could think about while sweating my way down the road was the next convenience store where I could buy a half gallon of ice-cold orange juice.

How much did I sweat on Route 82 headed into Waycross? It was so hot and humid that it was like pedaling inside a steam sauna. Sweat dripped from my scalp, before running down the back of my spine where it soaked into my shirt. From my forehead, it ran down into my glasses where it pooled on the rims. Some of it escaped down my nose where it dripped onto the top tube, then splattered onto my legs. Sweat hung from my chin and ear lobes until I shook it off. It ran down my arms, glistening through the hairs until it soaked my riding gloves. Rest stops made it worse when it dried and left salt cakes on my body and clothes.

Nonetheless, I was having a good time. A passing car's bumper sticker said it all: "A bad day of bicycling is better than a good day of work." It was true, I didn't mind the sweat because I was exploring the South. I'm not saying that it was scads of fun, nor was I in comfort, but at that moment in Georgia, that's the way it was--hot and miserable. I accepted it because to complain would be useless. It's times like that, especially on a bike, I just live; I accept the moment. That's the special intrigue of bicycle touring. Sure, I love riding on the flats on an autumn day. It's easy pedaling and the air is cool. I'm comfortable and dry. It sure beats busting my butt going up a 6,000-foot climb on a hot day. But there's the catch. The flats have their own beauty, but it doesn't compare to the mountains. Given the choice, I'd take the mountains even with the price of the climb.

That's the point—I accept the flats when they are happening, yet love the mountains when it's time for climbing. I couldn't change any of it at one moment anyway. I take it a day at a time.

No doubt about it that muggy day in South Georgia. I couldn't wait for a convenience store. I could buy their entire stock of orange juice. I felt dehydrated and I couldn't drink fast enough to replenish my fluids. Ahead on the left, I spotted a dilapidated paint chipped building kitty-corner to the pavement. Gray moss hung down the sides of the faded white paint and red dust lined the windowsills. Coke and Pepsi coolers with their colored logos stood like military sentries on both sides of a broken screen door.

Two faded red Texaco gas pumps with broken glass over the meters stood out in the sun. A bent tin roof provided shade for two long benches alongside the building. I looked like a dripping fountain as I rode up near the gas pumps and laid my bike against a pole. Two old men stared at me, but said nothing. Off to the side, a thin, gray haired black man in tattered clothes sat gumming his ice cream.

Seconds later the door slammed behind me, kicking up a dozen flies on the screen mesh. Inside, a dirty wood floor led past a huge lady sitting behind the counter, knitting a sweater. She wore a basketful of curlers in her hair, with three extra chins tumbling down from below her lips. I headed for the cooler.

"How ya'll today?" she asked.

"Just fine ma'am," I replied. "Sure am thirsty. Does it get any hotter than this?"

"You better believe it, son," she said. "Last week, it was 96 with the humidity over 90."

"How can you stand it?" I asked.

"The weather is like the flies," she replied. "You can't do nothin' about 'em, so you just get used to 'em."

"I guess you're right," I said. "Do you have any half-gallons of OJ? I only see quarts."

"What ya'll see is what ya'll git."

"You got any cookies?"

"Yes sir, near the bread on the second isle over."

I paid for two quarts of orange juice and a bag of chocolate chips. Seconds later, the screen door slammed behind me, kicking up the flies again. An old geezer had pulled up to the pumps and was filling his pickup with gas. He complained about the heat. The two old men continued staring at me in silence. I wondered if they were alive.

After swigging the first quart, I inhaled a handful of cookies. A mongrel dog got up from behind the Pepsi cooler, walked over and sniffed me. He looked at my bag of cookies with pleading eyes. "Okay buddy, here's one for you, but that's all you get, unless you want to pedal my bicycle down the road." I flipped him a cookie. He walked back to his hard wood bed and began crunching on his prize.

I grabbed the orange juice and belted down half the jug. The cold liquid slid down my throat and filled my stomach. After chomping down on a second handful of cookies, I noticed my chain was dry. I tossed the bag of cookies onto the pack along with the second jug of orange juice. After unzipping my tool pouch, I grabbed the spray can and spun the crank backwards. The chain rolled through the pulleys and threaded its way around the freewheel, and back toward the middle chainring. Most of the lengths were dry.

"You gotta' check this chain more often," I muttered to myself. "This chain's dry as a bone."

I sprayed both pulley axles and drenched the freewheel. I cranked the pedals backwards slowly, spraying the chain as it came off the lower pulley. No matter how careful I was, oil sprayed onto the rim. As I squatted there, sweat dripping down from my brow and chin, the black man shuffled toward me. I was nearly done when he stood over me.

"Ever change the oil in yer' knees?" he mumbled.

"What?" I asked, looking up at him.

"You ever change the oil in yer' knees?" he repeated more clearly.

At first, I didn't know how to answer, but then I thought about it saying, "Only when they squeak, sir."

He laughed through his gums. The last of his ice cream cone vanished into his mouth.

"How far has you ridden that bicycle anyways?"

"From the Golden Gate Bridge in San Francisco." I said.

"Naw! You ain't gonna' tell ole' Charlie a lie now are ya'?" he said. "The devil gonna' take you if you don't tell the truth now ya' hear?"

"It's true, I rode this bicycle starting from the Golden Gate Bridge. I've been on the road three months. It's no big deal. Lots of people have ridden across America on a bicycle."

"Well, I'll be hanged," he said. "I never dreamed a man could ride across this whole country."

"Some people have ridden a bicycle around the world."

We got to talking, ole Charlie and me. This 91-year-old man, wearing tattered clothes, was the son of a slave who was freed by Lincoln back in 1865. This toothless man, with clouded black eyes, yet a clear mind, possessed more historical knowledge than a history book. His father was brought over to America in chains on a slave ship to pick cotton in the Carolinas.

When things heated up over the abolitionist movement, his father was sold to a tobacco grower in Waycross. After the Civil War, things didn't change much for his father, except he got married and fathered five children. Charlie was the youngest. He never went to school and to this day couldn't read or write. He had worked on farms all his life and had outlived his wife and four kids, save one.

He felt that Franklin D. Roosevelt was the greatest president, but he wished that Jesse Jackson would one day would live in the White House. If Jesse couldn't make it, then Bill Cosby would make a good second choice, to keep some humor in politics.

This intriguing old man captivated me for an hour. He was an enthusiastic, walking, talking history book. He hadn't been out of the county in his 91 years, but he had listened to radio, then television, and stored everything he had learned in a lucid memory. As he talked, a pattern of his life and his attitude illuminated every historical perspective. What held my attention was his span of reference. He was born in 1889 before electricity, before cars, before paved roads. In his time, he had seen the entire modern world develop with unbelievable speed.

"What was the greatest moment of your life?" I asked.

"There was such a great many moments Charlie has seen, but maybe when Mr. Neil Armstrong walked on the moon, that has to be the greatest moment of Charlie's life," he said. "All his life, Charlie has been lookin' up at that ole man in the moon, but when Mr. Armstrong walked on it, well, that was the greatest moment."

"How about the worst?"

"Lotta' worsts young fella'," he said. "These many years later, Charlie can't figure out why human beings has to keep hurtin' each other."

"What's the most important thing in life?" I asked.

"After good health, it's got to be love. You gots to love someone. An someone gots to love you."

Later, Charlie departed with his 70-year-old son. I watched as they sped away down the dusty dirt road leading into the Georgia back country.

The next day, I reached the Atlantic Ocean. My coast-to-coast adventure ended, but Charlie and dozens of other people convinced me that nothing ends until you die. Without question, living is an attitude manifested by spirit.

Bicycle touring is the spiritual vehicle for adventure that I call traveling at the 'human speed.' It beats the measured pace of walking, yet surpasses in quality experiences the alacrity of 60 mile per hour. You can smell the flowers along the way. You own the day and the road leads you to anywhere in the world. Along the way, some of the people you meet, share the simplest, truest truths in life. Have I ever changed the oil in my knees?

Only when they squeak.

If these stories grabbed your interest, you might like the entire 60-chapter anthology of my most 'epic' moments on six continents over 45 years of bicycle travel. You may find it on Amazon.com—**Bicycling Around the World: Tire Tracks for Your Imagination** by Frosty Wooldridge

Chapter 23

HOPES AND DREAMS—YOUR RETIREMENT YEARS

"All of us carry our hopes and dreams in our hearts and minds. We've enjoyed a lifetime of two-week trips that worked up to four weeks if we stayed with the same job. But now, in our "Golden Years", we've got unlimited time to fulfill our dreams. Some of us love to travel by boat, sail, train, plane, canoe, mountain climbing, rafting, skiing, kayaking, parasailing and a dozen other modes of adventure. This array of my friends graciously presented their hopes and dreams. They might give you ideas. Some of them have ridden bicycles long distances. Others would like to ride long distances. You might pick up some of their ideas and make them your own." FHW

FRANK: ENGINEER, TRIATHLETE, FATHER, ADVENTURE SEEKER

Like most people, I'd been building a bucket list for many years while I toiled away at the missile factory that I worked at for 28 years. Many people express a desire to travel in retirement, myself included. I've always been a driven person. I've completed two full ironman distance triathlons and put myself through college while working full time and raising a family.

I've been a cyclist for many years and have always said "when I retire,

I'm going to ride my bicycle across the U.S." As an aerospace engineer I was very familiar with measuring things, schedules. and budgets. In January of 2016 I retired at the age of 59 years old. Being an engineer, I, of course planned out my trip across the U.S. The schedule was very detailed with each day's distance and possible camp spots etc.

I remember one day riding north up the coast of California with a really strong headwind. I was driving myself hard to make it to my planned destination. I was more focused on my plan than in just enjoying the journey. It was just the first in many lessons I learned from that trip. I was on a path of personal growth that I believe has made me a better person. Although it took me some time to let go of the schedule, once I did, I found myself free to enjoy just being right here right now in the moment.

As a triathlete I was used to measuring my distance, time, what I ate, anything that would affect my overall time. My job had me dealing with schedules and budgets. But, out here on the road there was no sense of the hurried pace of my prior life. Once I stopped trying to control everything and just let life happen, I started to see the world differently. I threw away the schedule and started to focus more on the journey itself.

I had started the trip with the goal of riding my bike across the U.S. What an athletic accomplishment right, no it's not really about that. Seeing national parks, historical places and places of unbelievable beauty is amazing and I accomplished that also. But, what I really discovered was the relationships of the people I met along the way was the unintended reward of this journey. The journey truly is the reward! I am so grateful for the memories of all the generous, loving, kind folks who have helped me with everything from a bed and a meal to a ride to the next bike shop to fix my broken bike. I've met so many people who told me they were living vicariously through me. I always give these people a word of encouragement that people shouldn't be afraid to get out and experience the world in which we all live. I met and rode with many other cyclists who are still my friends to this day and will always be there for me.

These are the type of people who live life everyday enjoying the simple pleasures of a sunrise, a hug from a friend, the birds singing in the trees, the mountains, the rivers, the beaches, and everything wonderful and beautiful in this great world of ours. These gifts are free. There is no charge at all to open your eyes, heart and mind to everything around you.

I know that not everyone my age (63) can physically do some of the activities that I enjoy. There are no words to describe the feeling of skiing down from the top of a mountain through the trees on a bluebird powder day or backpacking to an alpine lake and sitting around the campfire singing songs with good friends. These are my retirement dreams, maybe yours are different. The really important thing to do in retirement is to have dreams.

Build that bucket list and it doesn't need to include a trip to Peru to see Machu Picchu. Maybe your retirement dream includes volunteering at the senior center or spending time with the people you love. Maslow's hierarchy of needs consists of a five-stage pyramid with the top-level being self-actualization. In retirement when all the other human needs have been met its the time for self-actualization, learning to paint or playing a musical instrument or help your fellow man through volunteering. This may be your adventure; the key is to find something that really jazzes you and make that happen.

Retirement is really amazing. I am truly blessed with a great life. I love to ride my bicycle around town or around the country. A motorcycle trip to the east coast, I'm did it, skiing in the winter, I have a season pass, a road trip to visit friends and family with a visit to a national park, absolutely. Although I still have the responsibilities of my 96 y/o father, two sons and three grandchildren, these are the blessings of retirement. Being able to spend time with family and friends with whatever time we have left is one of the great joys of being retired. So, whatever your hopes and dreams may be for retirement, get out there and foster those relationships that make life worth living! Never stop dreaming about your next adventure.

Our coming into existence is highly unlikely but our death is certain. That point may seem clearer today, but what it really means - life or death - is up to us. I have long thought that it's a waste of time to ask, "What is the meaning of life?" It's you!

DAVE: MY CYCLING LIFE, BEFORE, DURING AND AFTER CROSSING THE USA

Back in the 1989 when I was only 42 years old, I saw thousands of people of all shapes and sizes, on bicycles pedaling through my town on what I later discovered was the yearly Dublin to Belfast mara-cycle ride. It was exactly 100 miles from Dublin to Belfast and then the same distance back to Dublin the next day. They all seemed to be enjoying themselves, chatting, laughing and all had a number on their backs and it was the site of all these people collectively going in one direction that started my interest in cycling, although I hadn't ridden a bicycle for over 20 years I just wants to be part of this. Together with my friend Bernard, we purchased two cheap road bikes and started cycling in the evenings at weekends, putting in lots of miles but never sure if we were training correctly, using the gears correctly or looking back, even eating correctly but in 1990 we registered for the Dublin – Belfast mara-cycle my first ever cycling event.

The feeling of having accomplished this 200-mile trip, the extasy of coming over the finishing line and wanting to do it again led to cycling becoming my "drug of choice." I would cycle nearly every hour available . Over the years I purchase better bikes, better clothes and took part in hundreds of events, none of them actual races but I always wanted to complete the event in the best time possible (and of course ahead of my friends).

I also met new friends through cycling and most of them are still my best friends today. Over the years we cycled together all over Europe, across the Alps and the Pyrenees from the top to the bottom of Italy, around France and many other places as well as navigating the rugged coastline of our beloved Ireland. We enjoyed each other's company, laughed a lot, drank a lot, sang a lot and of course have seen a lot of incredible places and experienced some unforgettable times with fellow travelers and complete non-cycling strangers.

Deciding to cycle across the USA in 2013 at the age of 64 was I suppose the result of wanting to see if all my cycling experiences over the past 22 years would give me the strength and mental capacity to cycle across a large continent, 4,100 miles to be competed in less than 80 days. This had always been something I wanted to try and together with my pal Gerry, we set off from Yorktown, Virginia on May 3, 2013 on what would turn out to be the best cycle adventure of my life. I wrote a book called "Cycling Across America, Journey of a Lifetime" because I just wanted to record our daily adventures, the places we went and the people we met, among them was "Frosty" who had been a good friend ever since we spent six days cycling together and who asked me to write a piece for his new book.

There were far too may outstanding, memorable and "not to be forgotten" experiences during this incredible 80 days but here are a few some good, some not so good.

Virginia –May 3rd . Being taken to the home of a complete stranger to be fed and watered and allowed to camp in his back garden, an act of outstanding kindness. Staying one night in the worst hotel in the world. Sleeping in a church. Grits. Music session in a bike shop in Damascus. Surprised to see so much poverty.

Kentucky – Being chased by packs of dogs. Using pepper spray for the first time. So many churches. Turtles crossing the road. Dry states. Chewing tobacco.

Illinois – Home of Popeye. The Mississippi River.

Missouri – Most frightening rainfall and thunderstorm ever. The Shaven Beaver Saloon. Seeing my first Hummingbirds.

Kansas – Hot. Big. Cattle fattening factories. Smell of manure. Oil wells. Cycling at 5.30 am to avoid the heat. Broken wheel and super mechanic. Tornado shelters. Feeling completely exhausted.

Colorado – The Rockies. Irish brown ale. Forest fires. Bill's collectables in Guffey. Hoosier Pass. Hot Silver Springs. German prisoners of war. Seeing no Moose. Continental Divide.

Wyoming - Windy. Sandstorms. The devastation of Jeffery City. The sadness of Byron who lives there. Bad times for the Indians. The Tetons. Yellowstone Park.

Montana – Quake Lake. Hunting, fishing and animal skins. Earthquakes. Virginia City. Gun and cigar shop. Mosquitoes. Temperature over 100 F. Red Indian escape route.

Idaho – Buffalo trails. 99 miles of winding road. Lowell, population 23. Fiddle Creek Fruits.

Oregon - Baker City. John Day. Picture Gorge. John Day (again)Faith, Hope and Charity. McKenzie Pass. Ice cold drinks. Hazelnut farms. Covered bridges. Florence. July 22.

So, having been cycling for the past 27 years, here are my personal thoughts and observations on some aspects of cycling long distances.

Cycling brings you a pure exclusive and overwhelming joy. It's a great feeling of freedom and wellbeing as your legs propel you along long distances and to new destinations. The soft "hum" of your tires on the road, the pleasure of taking a sip of drink on a really hot day. The small beads of salty sweat that make their way through your bandana and roll down to the tip of your nose and into your crossbar. The moment you reach the summit of a really hard climb and you click into a slightly higher gear at the second you reach the top.

The uplifting feeling you get when a tail wind picks you up and you are propelled effortlessly forward at great speed. Knowing that the burning muscular pain of a long hard climb will be instantly forgotten on the descent and the next day. The expectation of cycling around an uncharted bend not knowing what is around the corner.

Hearing heavy rain on the outside of your tent, knowing you're safe and dry. Fixing a puncture and immediately finding somewhere to wash your hands. The smell of a new inner tube. Knowing that you can cycle over 80 miles day after day after day. Meeting new people, be it other cyclists, other travelers or just folks you just meet along the way. Having a shower and a cold beer after a long cycle. Finding out what is making that annoying "clicking" noise on your bike and eliminating it.

I'm in my seventieth year now and as I type this, I am preparing for a cycle across Asia starting in January. I can't wait! That's what cycling does to you. It becomes part of your life, your heart and soul, and once mounted and riding your bicycle, you become at one with yourself, the world and with a little bit of imagination the universe.

Being a person who is also involved in helping people less fortunate than myself, last year (2019) I managed to secure a trishaw, which is a bicycle with two passenger seats in front. With this bike, I pick up older people who live in nursing homes and take them for a "spin" around our town, something they really enjoy and appreciate. This is good for them and good for me. Cycling has undoubtedly made my life exceptionally fulfilling and now I can use cycling to help others. What a total gift!

TOM: VETERAN BICYCLE TOURING LEADER

There is nothing inherent in an incident that dictates its meaning. "Meaning" is determined by each person. We are both the ultimate judge and the accused. You yourself must be the examiner. Did you do well, or did you squander your precious existence?

Kipling said, "If you've never been in the pit, you can never know the true pleasure of the summit." The thing is, when you ride a bike hundreds and hundreds of miles over the course of weeks you really are experiencing the pain, you really are descending a mountain at 50 mph with a freezing wind chill, or when you're in the desert getting baked and dehydrated, you're not dreaming it - you are in the desert getting dehydrated. There's a surreal aspect that's brought on by the pain, by the sore muscles, sore bum, bad roads, and outdoor accommodations. You have to face your deepest fears.

The only way you're ever gonna' know how strong you are as an individual is to put yourself in an extreme situation and see how you handle it. You do not know what's going to happen, and in our world that creates fear. It takes you down - past the success and the money and the comfort to a place that requires courage to enter. You prove it to yourself. The courage to show up when you can't control the outcome.

On a bicycle tour, you leave normal behind. It's an ego stripping thing: you get in touch with yourself by getting away from the ego. You haven't slept as much as you wanted to, you're not as clean as you'd like to be, but there's this energy building inside you that outstrips all that and you go forward - and when you finish, you never go back to the exact place you started. [You never regret the journey you took!]

Resilience is born out of the challenges we choose to meet.

When you ride endurance tours you are forced to confront your deepest fears. Can you stay on the bike and continue even though you're hurting, even though you're dazed and unsure, even though you can quit at the next town and be done instead?

It's an archetype of all human story telling in every culture on earth: indeed, even all the world's great religions have a character that goes through great suffering and gains some sort of spiritual advancement from that suffering.

If the nature of human life is suffering, then the way we deal with it and how we overcome it and grow, defines us.

A great quote: "A long stretch of road will teach you more about yourself than a hundred years of quiet." Patrick Rothfuss

REX: EXTENSIVE TRAVELER, CYCLIST ACROSS AMERICA, DREAMER

Retirement for the first 67 years of my life never dawned on my mind. Wish I had taken better care of my nutrition and exercise regimen. But I am now! Then, out of the blue, I was forced into retirement at 67 from the North Sea oil platforms. And reality came crashing down on me.

For certain, I lived a life of alternative living. After college, I traveled through 50 states and 30 countries. Truck driving for the summer, bartending and skiing for the winter in Colorado. School and skiing in Switzerland. Around the world and hard rock drilling in Australia. I got married and changed everything with a move to Norway. I drove a fish truck to Italy and Spain. But I focused on North Sea oil platforms for an end of career job. And along the way, many journeys on a motorcycle in North America, Europe and Australia.

A bicycle ride across America seemed like a good way to travel one summer. And many of the destinations one reads about in current and past publications. They are out there; so go see them. I liked to go on a motorcycle, too. Alaska five times, all of Europe including the eastern bloc many times. Fifty states many times. Australia a couple of times. Pamplona, Sturgis, The Havasu, Calgary, Highway 1, New Zealand, the Barrier Reef dives. Colorado Elk hunts. Actually, the list is as long and many as pretty much one man can do in 72 years.

And now, this retirement 'thing'. What do you do with so much time on your hands? Well, the list and plans get even more exotic. A new job in a gun store. Build a resort for bow hunting in the woods of Michigan. Another motorcycle trip to Alaska. A new job leading Norwegians around USA on a motorcycle. Winter ski trips.

And along the way always, old friends and new ones to meet. For me, the destinations are as thrilling the first time as the 5th or 10th time. It is not the destination; it is the journey. It is not the years; it is the miles. It is packing up the bike in Michigan or Norway or Australia. And a big smile, a look to the north or south or east or west. Ready, set, go! Another big smile and put it in gear. And ride.

So for me, retirement is a very illusive concept. A whole lifetime of this planet, what a wonderful opportunity to go and do and see. Work took up much time for most of those years but there was always time to choose as best you could. And then comes "retirement" and still it is a choice as best you can make.

I intend to choose well from now till the end of the journey. Good nutrition and even more exercise. Always positive thinking! Always an adventurous thought of, somewhere, something, go and see and do. We get this lifetime and this journey only once. No Mulligans! Use it and make it worth it. Make it a good ride. Experience how far you can go, how hard, how hot, how cold, how long, how beautiful, how inspiring. Maybe the word is, how "meaningful" you can make this journey.

What a planet, what a journey, what a ride. Whatever you do, you may not be able to do it next year. Do it this year. Do it now! Retire the day you die. And maybe just maybe, we do it again. And if not, we did it this time. Good travels to us all.

DAVID: TRAVELER, SKIER, ENTREPRENEUR, CYCLIST, BACKPACKER

In my 69th year, I cycled down the Continental Divide from Glacier National Park to Evergreen, Colorado. It was an epic adventure start to finish. How fortunate I was to have such an inspirational and knowledgeable friend along for the ride. He even let me use his bike that he used to travel from the bottom of South America to the Arctic Ocean.

Although I've ridden on numerous organized cycling trips, carrying all of your camping and cycling gear, clothing, food and water, etc. on your bike adds an entirely different level of difficulty to your trip. However, you're ready for anything which is quite liberating as you can travel at your own pace or as some riders call it, *the pleasure pace*. For example, we had such a nice time in Great Falls, Montana we spent one day at the Charles Russell Museum and the next at the Lewis and Clark Interpretive Center located on the Missouri River where they had such difficulty portaging the waterfalls. I recommend both of these as they added so much to the richness of our trip. After all, it's more about the journey than the destination, at least when you're a cycling road warrior.

I retired four years ago after being a workaholic for most of my life and seamlessly shifted, no pun intended, from one happy adventure to the next. I don't regret the work component as it gives balance to life, but the cool thing about being retired is the flexibility to do pretty much what you want, when you want.

If you're healthy and fit, then keep moving and keep trying new things for as long as possible.

Bottom line is that we don't have as much time as we like to think we do and despite all of the challenges and negativity out there, it's a beautiful world and aren't we the fortunate ones!

DEB AND DAVID: ENGINEERS, ACUPUNCTURISTS, NUTRITIONISTS, HEALTH LEADERS

In our late 40's and 50's we began acquiring real estate as a continuing source of income in our retirement. We went through the 2008 real estate bubble bust and lost most of it, but thankfully we retained a few properties in Colorado.

Oh, and then there's this thing called "Retirement". What does THAT really mean to us? Well, we are active in mind and body. We love what we do! I do NOT see retirement as a lack of meaningful work. David would like to enjoy less structure and more freedom to study, so for him that may, eventually become less time in the office.

In his fifties, David bicycle-toured from Croatia to Holland. He's toured with one of his friends through Colorado and Utah. Each time, it changed him spiritually and mentally. For the better!

Oh, and I'm a recording artist now. I'm told that, in the industry, I have what's called a pure voice. Who knew! The creation of these meditation recordings is part of a beautiful Journey in the spiritual realm, and I feel connected with the world on a different and magical level.

Last item: So how do we plan to live the rest of our lives? I've already alluded to some of it. David wants to study physics. And as a long-time engineer, he will undoubtedly enjoy inventing things, too. It's in his nature. **Ah....and we will travel more.**

BOB AND MARIE: CHRYSLER EXECUTIVE, LIONS CLUB, TRAIN SETS, GRANDKIDS, CYCLING ACROSS AMERICA

My retirement plan was simple. Stop working at 55; start the last chapter of this lifetime. My dad didn't get his chance. Build a retirement home in a Colorado mountain community with a ski resort so our daughter and her future family will visit. Join Lions Club to make new friends. Enjoy outdoor activities. Outfit a home cabinet making shop. After that; see what happens; go with the flow, and be open to new challenges.

Someone once said to set a goal so big that you can't achieve it until you become the person who does it. Nineteen years into retirement, it is the challenges undertaken that become the spicy sauce on each day. A just-retired acquaintance was worried he'd sit around because he didn't have any hobbies. My advice was to undertake a big challenge. And after that one, look for another. Riding a bicycle down the northern Norway coastline for three weeks was my first big challenge.

The adventures kept coming for me after Norway. Bicycling across America, two knee replacements, then riding up the west coast of Michigan and then across Washington state and down the coast of Oregon. And, of course, RAGBRAI bicycling across Iowa. Being Vegan for a few years. Lots of cabinetmaking projects. Numerous officer positions with Lions Club. Restoring a 1949 Willy's Jeep. Building a train layout for the grandkids, lots of Lego projects and this summer a tree house for when they visit.

Retirement should be a series of challenging adventures for our final decades in this realm. Undertaking the adventures is not always easy but it will leave you proud. Think of it as periodic maintenance for your sense of personal worth. Your old boss won't be patting you on the back for a job well done...you have to do it yourself in retirement.

I frequently recall the words of coach Jimmy Dugan in the movie *A Team of Their Own*, "It's supposed to be hard. If it wasn't hard, everyone would do it. The 'hard' is what makes it great." Retirement isn't easy, it takes hard work, fill yours with personal challenges. You will enjoy a great life.

JIM AND KAREN: BUSINESSMAN, ATHLETE, NOVELIST, TRAVELER

I retired in November 2005 and moved from Southern California to the foothills of Denver, Colorado after a forty-year career with a major aluminum company. My wife and I moved seven times in the first thirteen years, all corporate moves; and I ended up traveling the world over the last fifteen years. My retirement formula modeled a mentor and former boss: he never came back while living only three miles from the offices. This wasn't out of any bitterness; he was the former president and didn't want to meddle in the new boss's efforts. More importantly, he was building a new life.

That's what I did: I built a new life—centered around staying healthy, challenging my mind, and making new friends. While my wife and I like to travel, and we've done so, I've had enough of airports in my life, so we have limited our travels to chosen special trips—Australia, New Zealand, France, Italy, Greece, Patagonia, and Hawaii fairly often.

As for my health, first of all, it could be said that in my former life, I was a once a year downhill skier, although I did a good bit of cross-country skiing back in Ohio, upstate New York, and on an adult Outward Bound expedition in Northern Minnesota in 1978. So, I bought a downhill season pass, skied a lot, and improved my skill level. I've skied every winter since, and with my late start at consistency, I'm not able to ski rough terrain, but I am capable of skiing long days on intermediate hills and enjoy it. I hope to ski well into my eighties.

Secondly, I was a former marathoner, USTA league tennis player, gym rat, and mountain biker in Southern California. In Colorado, I took up road biking, completing the Triple Bypass 120-mile bike ride at age seventy. Now at age seventy-seven, I ride the excellent trail system in the Denver area, with plenty of hills nearby, all year, depending on weather (about 2,500 miles per year). I also swim, hike, go to the gym, and take two yoga classes.

As for challenging my mind, I've written two novels, with one published, and only successful in that the people who have read it, liked it. It's truly okay since I have little interest in hawking my book. The enjoyment was in writing it and the challenge of making a good story. The other is in suspension—because I'm not certain what I want to do with it, since I'm afraid that I channeled Quinten Tarantino!

Secondly, I took up a musical instrument—the guitar. I took lessons for three years, and continue to play off and on to this day. I never had visions of performing in front of crowds or joining a band. My playing has been jazz focused, and always a form of therapy, relaxation, and learning something new—there's always something new to learn.

As for making new friends, we've certainly done that. We're both church goers, I sing in a choir, and I joined a group of church fellows for 6:30 a.m. coffee. I also belong to a group of a dozen men called Curmudgeons, with some PhD scientists where we meet every Thursday morning and solve the world's problems...which doesn't really happen because we're just talking amongst ourselves. I also have my biking friends. My wife and I also have a neighborhood circle of friends and others scattered about town. We also have family close by—a son, a daughter, and four grandchildren.

It's a wonderful life with good health, peace, and tranquility. I have a mantra, likely to change depending on circumstances, or not: I am calm, dispassionate, and reflective, but mindful of the world's bad news, my unsound thoughts, and my harmful feelings, the latter two being the only things I can truly control.

KAREN: HOUSEWIFE, WIDOW, CYCLIST

My life crashed when my husband exited the planet. As a widow, it was difficult and emotionally painful to pick up the pieces. Certainly, friends and family supported me, but I had to pick myself out of depression and decide what do with my life at 71.

Three months before my husband and I were about to embark on a coast to coast bicycle journey from San Francisco to Washington DC, he came down for breakfast, grabbed the paper and sat down to read. As I stood over the stove preparing breakfast, I heard a "thunk" on the kitchen table. I looked around to see my husband slumped over in his chair with his head on the table. He died of a heart attack.

After the funeral, I felt my life ended. But my friend Hattie asked me if I still wanted to ride across America. "Sure do," I said.

"Well, put an ad into Adventure Cycling Magazine for a "Companion Wanted," she said.

So, I did! I asked for a senior citizen male or female who wanted to camp when needed and motel a lot. I intended to ride each day comfortably with no set number of miles. I set the course from San Francisco to Washington DC. I said I was, "Easy to get along with, physically fit and well educated."

Within 24 hours, three women answered my ad. All of them widows! I chatted with each one of them individually. Each of them felt high spirited, excited to ride and, at the same time, mellow.

I gave them the most important ground rules:

1. No talk about race, religion or politics.
2. No complaining about the past or your husbands.
3. Get into leg-shape and saddle-shape before the ride.
4. Ride an E-Bike if you like.
5. If you have a problem with a fellow cyclist, speak civil and work it out. If need be, split from the group for a few days.
6. We encourage each other and enjoy the ride each day.
7. Safety at all times and keep your distance.
8. Know how to camp and be prepared if we can't find a motel.

The one thing about old age that I like is the fact that everyone carries the wisdom of a lifetime of trials, tribulations and heart break. At the same time, each of us calmed our egos and realized that "getting along" is more important than being "right."

We took a group picture at the Golden Gate Bridge. During the first week of the ride, we worked out the kinks. We took a zillion photographs and shared our life stories. We met many women on the road who lamented, "You're living my dream."

At the Lincoln Memorial in Washington DC, we shared another

group photograph. To this day, those women are my sisters and we cherish our cycle journey as the most 'epic' experience of our lives. Not one of us regretted that we took a chance and experienced that incredible journey across America. My husband's spirit accompanied me the entire trip.

PAUL: TEACHER, MUSICIAN, FATHER, WIDOWER

My wife and I retired in our early sixties. We planned to travel until we died. Trouble is, she contracted cancer and passed away. It left me with a vacant heart and troubled mind. What do you do when your life-mate of 40 years passes on before you?

First of all, I dreamed of cycling across America, Europe and Canada. I thought I would be doing it with my wife Linda. She loved to bike tour with me. Losing her was the most painful experience of my entire life. Yes, our kids comforted me, but they had to get on with their own lives.

What did I do? First of all, I joined a "Meet-up" bicycle club in my City of Atlanta. Before I knew it, several other women in their sixties seemed to gather around my bike before and after every ride. Soon, we shared dinners. After taking a few rides, one of the women talked about riding across the USA. That perked me up. Plus, she was a great rider and pleasant on the eyes at 65.

After many dates, and lots of rides, I felt that we seemed compatible.

"Any chance you want to ride across America coast to coast with me, Paula?" I asked.

Without hesitation, Paula said, "Are you kidding me? Let's do it."

No, we're not married, but we made the ride. Next summer, we're headed over to Europe. Yes, she uses an E-bike so I can't keep up with her. What do I care? We're having a ball together.

What did I learn from my misfortune? If you're alive, you need to stick your nose out into life's possibilities. Feeling sorry for yourself takes you nowhere. Yesterday cannot be changed. You cannot live in the past or worry about what happened.

One of the practices I followed to escape my depression over the loss of my wife was to start singing my favorite songs when sad thoughts entered my head. The more I sang, the more my mind entertained more positive thought patterns.

I discovered that by enjoying the present and speaking in a positive way about the future, I attracted more people into more upbeat conversations. That was a huge lesson for me: leave the sad moments of my life in the past while I relish the present and make plans for the future. There's a poem by an unknown author that says: May the road rise up to meet you, may the wind be ever at your back. May the sunshine warm upon your face and the rain fall softly on your fields. And until we meet again, May God hold you in the palm of his hand.

JON AND CYNTHIA: LOVE LUXURY TOURING, EXOTIC COUNTRIES, GREAT FOOD

My husband and I love riding our bicycles. We also love motels, restaurants, clean riding clothes and daily showers. When we retired, many of our friends expected us to ride across America, Europe and Australia.

But we didn't know the first thing about long distance touring. One of our friends bought us a complimentary year's subscription to Adventure Cycling Magazine. The stories from around the world intrigued us. A lot of them told about hardships, rain, cold and difficult riding across mountains, deserts and nasty conditions. We're not the camping type, so that kind of adventure didn't interest us.

Luckily, at the back of the magazine, we found cycle touring companies that offered one-week rides across different states and two-month rides across America. We discovered the Erie Canal Ride, Blue Ridge Skyline Drive Ride, Natchez Trace, Katy Trail, Lewis & Clark Trail, Columbia River Gorge Trail, and many more from a week to a month. Biggest plus for us: motels, fine foods and total support.

To our delight, we discovered the "Bike and Barge" trips in Europe. We took a three-week barge trip on the Rhein River. Another on the Danube River. We met dozens of other senior riders who loved seeing the sights every day at different locations. We enjoyed fabulous breakfasts. The touring company gave us maps for local attractions, lunch stops and historic places to visit. We enjoyed local cuisine before coming back to the barge where we shared whine, cheese and brunch with all our new friends. During the night, the barge took us to the next attraction.

Some companies offer "women only" tours across America and all over Europe. Really, there is something for everyone.

For all those touring companies, they offer custom bike fitting, E-bikes and full support at all times. We plan to make many more reservations around the world. Next ride—New Zealand!

Retirement: don't you just love it!

ROBERT AND MARSHA: ARTIST AND CYCLIST, RETIRED, HAPPY TRAILS

Marsha and I got married right out of college. While in school, we loved parties, movies and dancing. We got along extremely well. But what we didn't know was the problem of different incompatibilities such as I loved to bicycle and camp. She loved fine restaurants and five-star hotels. Being young and naïve, we simply didn't consider those factors. We were polar opposites.

A funny thing happened on the journey toward our lives together. At first, we thought 'love' would carry us through our problems. After having two kids, my love for being on my bike got displaced by our children for the next 25 years. Their needs superseded my needs.

We struggled along. We kept it together. After the kids graduated from college, we became DINK's. Duel income no kids. Marsha revved up her artistic talents and I revved up my bicycle riding. We found happiness in our separate avenues of expression.

At age 65, we retired. At my local bicycle club, one of the guys befriended me. He had the same challenges with his wife. She loved jewelry making. He loved bicycling. In fact, before he got married, he bicycled across the USA from San Francisco to Virginia Beach, Virginia.

"That was the greatest time of my life," he said. "I want to do it again. Wanna' go with me?"

"Hell yes," I said. "But I've got to figure out something with Marsha. She would never take that ride."

"Tell you what," Paul said. "Let's get our wives together. Let's put them into a motorhome with a trailer filled with their art stuff. Each can pursue their creativity daily on the trail. We can ride all day, stop for the night with them, and they can paint and create jewelry all the way across America."

Our wives loved the idea of crossing the country in a motorhome to see the sights and refresh their creative juices. Thankfully, they got along like two peas in a pod.

In 2019, we started out of Florence, Oregon and headed to Savannah Beach, Georgia. Something magical happened. Paul's wife, Jackie began selling her jewelry along the route. She sold out daily because her jewelry was exquisite. My wife Marsha started paintings on 12" X 16" and 16" X 20" canvases that we stored in the trailer of the motorhome. She painted incredible landscapes and small-town main streets. If she didn't finish the painting during the day, she took a picture of the scene to make sure she remembered the details within the painting. Later, she finished the landscape.

By the time we left California, our wives were making quite a bit of money. To tell the truth, they nearly paid for the entire trip including renting the motor home, food, gas and camping fees.

What was even more interesting was the fact that they grew their creative talents 10-fold while they loved spending time together. Paul and I smiled every day because we were doing what we loved, and our wives loved what they were doing.

At the end of the trip when we touched our front wheels into the Atlantic Ocean, Paul's wife Jackie said, "Let's do this again…in Europe."

Paul looked at me and I looked back at him, "I think we can arrange that…."

ALEX: TOTAL LIFE CHANGE FROM OBESE TO LEAN, RIDE ACROSS AMERICA, EUROPEAN TOUR

As with many baby boomers after college, I got drafted into the U.S. Army. I struggled through basic training at Fort Benning, Georgia. Then, Advanced Infantry Training at Fort Polk, Louisiana. I got shipped out to Vietnam in 1968 during the Tet Offensive. I didn't expect to live through it. I stood 6'1" inches and 180 pounds. I was in outstanding physical condition.

Somehow, a bullet or bomb didn't have my name on it. When I returned, I got into corporate. I worked my tailfeathers off for 35 years, made a lot of money, bought the big house, married a beautiful woman, fathered two wonderful kids and lived the American Dream.

At 65, with the kids through college, I decided to retire and live one of my youthful dreams—to ride a bicycle across America. But I had several big problems. I had smoked my whole life and I was an alcoholic. To top that off, I went from 180 pounds in college to 280 pounds at the age of 65.

An old college friend of mine said he would ride across America because he was going to retire in two years. I was excited. "Can I ride with you?" I said.

He said, "Alex, there's no way you can ride a bike across America. You're so fat, you wouldn't make it two days without your rear-end killing you from so much pressure pain on the seat. You wouldn't be able to walk let alone ride. Plus, you could end up with a heart attack."

"What if I lose it by the time you retire?" I asked.

"If you get down to 180 and pass a stress test," he said. "We could ride."

"You got it," I said.

From that moment onward, I found the most motivation to accomplish something I had in the back of my mind for my whole life. My wife supported me one hundred percent.

I got into AA and within a month, I stopped drinking. I never looked back. I took a drug called Chantix to bring my smoking down to zero. Then, I got on a Vegan diet with a top natural-pathic doctor, who was also a cyclist. I joined a riding club. I became obsessed with losing weight. I became more disciplined than at any other time in my life. I stayed with my daily calorie consumption of 1,500 per day. I pedaled into faster and faster group rides to burn more calories. I wanted that ride across America. My wife wanted the ride for me. My kids wanted me to succeed.

Two years later, I walked into the bon voyage party at exactly 180 pounds. My friend Wayne walked over to me, "You're ready." I replied, "You bet your sweet ass I am!"

My wife walked up to Wayne, "Thank you for saving my husband's life."

As I write this story of the latter part of my life, tears run down my cheeks. In front of me on my desk, I have an 8"X10" picture of my friend Wayne and me with our fists raised in triumph on the Atlantic Ocean. I swear, it was the greatest moment of my life.

And I can say that bicycling across America was the most memorable and epic experience in my life. The Mojave Desert, the Rocky Mountains, the Great Plains, the Appalachian Mountains, the heat, the rain, the winds and the magnificent challenges provided everything I needed for such a tremendous bicycle adventure. The people we met and the sights we saw on the ride, well, just beyond incredible. And, now, with an E-bike, my wife and I ride together. In 2018, we toured Europe.

If I could lose 100 pounds to make my dreams come true, I am here to say that anyone can change his or her life to live the fantasy. My advice: just decide to do it, and then, go do it!

Chapter 24

EVERYTHING YOU NEED TO KNOW FOR LONG-DISTANCE BICYCLE ADVENTURE

"Riding a bicycle flat out brings joy throughout a person's mind, body and spirit. Pedaling scintillates every cell in one's body toward some kind of nirvana, state of grace and/or total bliss. It might be deemed something like the ancients equate to enlightenment. Whatever you call it, the feelings ring from the rafters of your mind. Everyone enjoys that smile on your face and in your spirit when they meet you on tour on your bicycle." FHW

GETTING STARTED
THE RIGHT BIKE

Everyone carries a bias about something dear to his or her heart. When it comes to bicycle touring, I've tried various approaches to equipment. Many of my lessons have been learned the hard way. Experience proves a stern taskmaster. I've stood in rainstorms with a breakdown, wondering why I hadn't listened to a friend who had been through it. Maybe I didn't listen because I thought I knew it all. Wrong! Even with miles and years behind my wheels, new ideas pop up daily. I'm willing to learn from other riders, because each one has a different style that incorporates something better into his or her bicycle touring operation.

Ben Franklin said it best: "Penny wise, pound foolish."

That wisdom holds true to this day. It applies to the bike you buy, and your gear.

More than once, I've been asked for advice on what kind of bike to ride. Am I biased? You bet. My inclination for bikes and equipment comes from a long trail of mistakes. You may obtain a host of experts' opinions, and they are valid relative to each person's needs, and aspirations in touring.

Light touring machine or heavy mountain bike?

Hands down—buy a mountain touring bike. It's the best thing to happen to bicycle touring either nationally or internationally. Cost? If you're touring plans mean two weeks per year in the USA, buy a bike in the $600.00 range. For international tours of six months duration, spend $1,500.00 or more and save money in the long run. For those who want the best, a custom-built mountain touring bike will cost $2,500.00 to $4,500.00. It's a lot of money and it's a lot of bicycle.

Some will tell you that a mountain bike is too heavy. Baloney! We're talking five pounds more at the most. That goes for women or men. You won't feel the weight. They say it handles harder. No way. Your body adapts to any load. That bike will become as comfortable as your favorite easy chair.

Why a mountain bike? First of all, comfort levels increase because of the fat tires. Buy ridged 1.75 tires for a smooth ride. A mountain bike offers a better, softer ride. You don't get front-end shimmy from being overloaded in the panniers or handlebar bag. Another big plus is the rarity of flat tires on a mountain bike. I've gone five months without a flat. No conventional touring bicycle can boast that. Those 1.25-inch tires get cut or worn out much too often. I love the security of knowing my tires are sturdy, especially on a long downhill, high-speed coast. Additionally, you can load a mountain bike up with tons of weight and not worry about spokes breaking (26 inch versus 27 inch rims), or wheels warping out of true. Best tire: Schwalbe Marathon Plus Tour.

Customize that mountain bike for touring. Replace the straight bars with wide drop bars or butterfly bars. That will give you three hand holding positions. Buy an Aero bar that will give you a place to rest your forearms and take you over the front of the bike for hours of comfortable riding. That means your shifting levers must be relocated on the down tube, or bar end shifters are available. Install a 40-spoke rear wheel, if available, for added endurance, especially for international touring. Buy the heaviest gauge, highest quality spokes for that back wheel, and make certain the person who builds your wheel knows what he/she is doing. Check around and get several opinions. By investigating, you will discover the best bike person in your town. Be aware of fast talkers who seem to know it all. Ask them how much and where they have toured. Do they know how to fit a bike to your body? Make sure they do it. Learn how to do it yourself. It's important to get a perfect fit. Your enjoyment depends on it.

Two items in the drive train stand out as the very important to me. I install a front Granny gear 24 tooth chain ring with a 34-tooth low end freewheel gear. No sense killing yourself on climbs. Best rear derailleur? I won't go anywhere without a Deore XT. That derailleur outlasts anything on the market.

For those who love 'light touring', yes, by all means buy a light touring bike. For women who want a lighter ride, yes, buy that bike that works for you. In the end, do your due diligence and buy the right bike for you.

You will develop your own style given a few miles, but it's nice to feel confident in your bicycle when you start out with a quality machine that fits your needs.

E-bikes: many great choices to give you and your spouse an extra lift while riding. Make sure you buy one with a kickstand and solid rear rack. My best advice: Hai-Bike with four speed-assist selections, excellent rack, 75 miles on one charge and solid German technology. My wife bought one and loves it. She completed the Lewis & Clark Trail on hers. Also, she rode the West Coast with it. Very dependable. Check with Consumer Reports on E-bikes to make sure you buy a dependable ride.

PREPARING FOR INTERNATIONAL BICYCLE TOURING

Going on a bicycle tour to some exotic country? Developing country? Whether you're going three weeks or six months, you have dozens of things to take care of before boarding the airplane. Preparing for an international tour is like battling a four-alarm fire. When you think one blaze is under control, another one needs immediate attention.

Begin preparing NOW—three to six months in advance. If you work forty or fifty hours a week, solid preparation will keep you from going crazy a week before departure. In my own world tours, I've found each continent needs specialized consideration. For example, in America, you can expect a bicycle shop in the next town if you need a spare part. In Africa, forget it. Whether you crank your bicycle across the Arctic Circle in Norway, push through the Andes Mountains in Peru, or sweat your way across the Nullarbor Plains of Australia—the success of your journey depends on what you do before you leave.

The key to that success is COMPLETION of your "To Do" and "To Buy" lists months before you leave. When you make your target date seven days to a month in advance of departure, you can relax at the bon voyage party without having an ulcer. Additionally, your health during the ride may depend on your advance preparation.

To make things easier on you, major and minor areas of concern will be covered. You may refer to "What to take and how to pack it," in this chapter. As you begin to acquaint yourself with the enormity of international touring preparation, get out a pen and a paper, and start a list.

BICYCLE AND EQUIPMENT

Two to three-week guided tours usually enjoy a sag wagon and mechanics to repair and maintain your bicycle. With those tours, your bike, whether you rent or bring your own, is not as critical a factor in the success of your tour. However, buy a bike and gear that will serve you well, so you may ride in confidence. Before going on tour, a basic tune up is a must. If you buy a new bike, be sure to ride it 300 miles and have the wheels trued. Be certain to have the bike fitted to your body.

For persons riding into developing world countries, a mountain bike, (converted for touring by adding drop bars or butterfly bars, 40 spoke hole hubs, extra quart water bottles, anatomical touring seat, aero bar, lower gearing, and fenders added) is highly recommended. It not only offers a superior ride on gravel roads; the tires last longer with far fewer flats. Make sure the quality of the bike and components matches the length of your ride. Insist on sealed bearings, but if you can't buy them, make sure your hubs have been overhauled. Carry tools that work with every part of your bike. Take a course in bicycle repair.

Highly recommended: In the past several years, those 'Aero' or 'Scott' bars have become vogue in racing circles because they lower the body resistance and create a bullet-like profile that is more streamlined. The big discovery for touring riders is a whole new form of comfort. By resting your arms on the bar, you rest your whole upper body and your butt. It allows for many more comfortable miles by taking the pressure off the triceps and shoulders. I highly recommend adding them to your comfort gear while on tour.

TENT, SLEEPING BAG, AIR MATTRESS AND COOKING GEAR

If you're on a guided tour, these items may not be important because lodging and food will be provided.

For those on individual tours, this equipment is extremely important. A quality, self-standing tent in the $250.00 to $350.00 range is a good bet. Be sure to seal the seams, carry extra seam sealer, and carry a waterproof ground mat.

A three-season sleeping bag at three pounds (down or fiberfill) good to 20 degrees Fahrenheit will keep you warm in most conditions. If you get caught at high altitude, you may wear your tights, mittens, sweater and cap to bed for extra warmth. The BEST air mattress is a 3/4 length self-inflating Thermo-Rest by Cascade Designs. I buy my gear at www.REI.com, www.LLBean.com, www.EMS.com, www.NorthFace.com because they give outstanding guarantees on their equipment.

Cooking gear includes a large pot, secondary pan, utensils, cups and a stove. Buy a stove that will burn many kinds of fuel for international destinations. An MSR International is one of the most popular and costs around $89.00. Talk with an REI employee for your specific needs and he/she will fill them. For the USA, a Coleman Primus with propane bottles works great.

DAY PACK OR SMALL BACKPACK

On top of your back rack, you may want to carry a 3,000 to 4,000 cubic inch capacity pack with three external pockets. It can be your utility pack for easy access to your camera, film, valuables and food. Carry your most often used gear in it. When stopping at a restaurant or whenever leaving the bike unattended for a few moments, you can release the bungee cords and sling the pack over your shoulders.

RAIN PROOFING YOUR GEAR

No doubt about it, you're at the mercy of the elements on a bicycle tour. Your equipment must be kept dry. Wrap everything in plastic bags. Keep your rain suit easily available. Make certain your film, digital cards and camera gear are securely rain proofed. Do the same for your sleeping bag and tent.

INTERNATIONAL TOURS

When riding in a foreign country, you're subject to different conditions. You may be vulnerable to infectious diseases, tainted food and water. You need extra precautions with eating, drinking and medicine. Boil, drop or filter your water, and eat only cooked foods. I use an MSR or First Need water filter. They are inexpensive and effective. Always peel fruits and vegetables. Wash your hands and keep your eating utensils clean. Drink only water you have filtered.

In a developing world country, you can expect a case of food poisoning at some point in your tour. Once you feel it coming on, induce yourself to vomit, and keep vomiting until your stomach is empty. Drink plenty of water to rinse out your system. This procedure will save you from prolonged suffering. If not food poisoning, you may pick up a new bacterium that doesn't agree with your intestines. In that case, you must tolerate the alien bugs until your system settles down to normal again.

Because you will not be able to bathe every day, carry anti-fungal ointment. Take a washcloth and wipe yourself down nightly with water. This will help prevent fungal growth on your skin. For poison ivy or skin rashes, carry Micatin cream. You can buy an MSR shower bag in order to take a three-minute shower every night.

Your passport is vulnerable to theft. Always keep it on your person or at arm's length.

IMMUNIZATION AND INOCULATIONS

Don't you love this category? It's a real pain in the rump, but necessary. Tell the nurse which countries you will be visiting and get your inoculations card completed with each shot or series. Take no chances with yellow fever, tetanus, typhoid, diphtheria or cholera. Insist on a Gamma Globulin shot for the best, but not perfect, prevention available for hepatitis.

Tell them how long you intend to tour, so they can adjust the dosage accordingly. Seek out all information you need in this area, and act upon it. Call or write the Center for Disease Control, U.S. Department of Health and Human Services. The number is in your local phone book under U.S. Government. Or, look up online! For shots, call your local hospital immunization department. If you demand answers, you will receive them. In this area, preparation and prevention are keys to your health.

Upon returning to the USA from a Developing world country, have a blood, urine and feces check to make sure you haven't picked up any liver flukes or other parasites. If tests are positive, begin treatment immediately.

In countries where malaria is present, you must start taking pills two weeks before leaving. With two or more people on the tour, take them on the same day, so everyone can remind each other during the ride. Follow instructions as your doctor tells you.

PASSPORT

This one can be a real hassle. Pick up the application at the post office. Fill it out and provide all documentation exactly as required. One mistake, and they will write you a letter with needed items for completion of your passport. In the meantime, your application is scattered between their office and your house.

Make certain you send them RECENT (within six months) official passport pictures and sign them on the back. Use those same pictures for visa applications. When applying for visas to different countries, use a travel agency's courier services. If you have any problems in processing, call your congressional representative. For peace of mind, make a list of the locations of American embassies in the countries you plan to visit.

Keep a dozen extra pictures for an international driver's license, hostel card and other needs that will pop up on an extended tour. Color, or black and white pictures are acceptable.

For extra precaution, take a photostat copy of your passport, driver's license and birth certificate. Put them in a separate compartment.

CAMERA EQUIPMENT

When the adventure ends, the pictures you snapped will be your most prized possessions. That is, if you didn't soak the camera in a rainstorm, or forget a spare light meter battery.

Camera gear needs special attention, whether you carry an expensive digital mirrorless or a sure shot automatic. Keep your card in a waterproof bag and insist that airport security people hand inspect it. Always ride with your camera in a plastic bag and out of the sun. Carry a small tripod.

CUSTOMS

Before leaving the states, have customs officers document U.S. ownership of your bike, camera equipment, expensive jewelry and any other gear you consider worth claiming as previously purchased property.

Otherwise, you could be liable for import taxes upon your return. Even more important, you could be charged more than $100.00 for an import tax in a developing world country!

NUTS AND BOLTS INFORMATION

Carry theft insurance for all your valuables overseas. Check with your insurance agent to make certain your bike and gear are covered.

Schedule a dental checkup and have everything in order before leaving. If you have a problem in a developing world country, you may suffer prolonged pain.

Money matters are very important. Purchase American Express traveler's checks because that company has the most offices throughout the world. Carry credit cards (Visa and Mastercard)that are honored internationally. Send your company $500.00 to $5,000.00 of debit credit, so you will have that to draw on if you're not back in time to pay a bill. You may need it in a pinch.

Make certain their expiration date is after your return. ALWAYS keep them in your money belt. I keep my passport and valuables on my person 24 hours a day and within arm's reach when taking a shower. When sleeping in a hostel, stuff your valuables into the bottom of your sleeping bag. Camera gear can go into the closed end of your pillowcase on your hostel sheet. NEVER assume your gear is safe from theft. It will be gone in seconds if left unattended.

For additional financial preparation, you can order foreign currency from your own bank. If you arrive in a country during a festival or other holiday, you will have at least $50.00 worth of their money for your immediate expenses. Carry a credit/debit card that you can plug into any ATM machine in most countries and retrieve needed money.

If there is any question as to safety, write the embassy of the country you want to visit. I avoided Columbia completely on my tour through South America. Hostile guerrilla action broke out on the routes I had to take to get to Ecuador. My body is allergic to bullets and jail, so I never take any chances. For complete information from USA sources, call the Citizen's Adviser Center in Washington, D.C. at phone number

(202) 647-5225; If a problem exists in a country, call (202) 647-6173; If a situation merits further investigation, call the Security Department, 24-hour command center at (202) 647-2412. Consider their suggestions seriously in your travel decisions.

Carry a booklet with addresses and phone numbers of embassies in a foreign country. Check in with the USA embassy staff and out when you leave a country.

DRUGS: Anyone who carries or consumes drugs in a foreign country is absolutely out of his or her mind. Jails in developing world countries are loaded with Americans who thought they wouldn't get caught. I can't stress this enough: STAY AWAY FROM DRUGS OR ANYTHING THAT LOOKS, FEELS OR SOUNDS SUSPICIOUS. If someone traveling with you carries drugs, insist he or she gets rid of the contraband. If they refuse, separate yourself from them. You may be considered an accomplice. Police in developing world countries lock you up and throw away the key.

Purchase your plane tickets two or three months in advance for possible discount prices, and assurance that you have a plane seat. Shop for an airline that charges least for a bicycle as extra baggage. Some airlines charge $150.00 for your bicycle ONE WAY.

Break your bike down and pack it into a sturdy box. Be sure to secure the front forks by placing a block of wood in the axle and tape it in place. Unscrew the rear derailleur from the dropout. Tape it to the chain inside some paper or a rag. That will save it from being bent. Or, have a shop do it for you. Be advised that you must know how to reconstruct your bike at destination, so learn how to break it down and put it back together.

Learn a few valuable phrases in the language of the country(s) you may visit. Learn to say "Hello, goodbye, good morning, good night, where is the toilet? How much? Yes, no, Mr., Mrs., please and thank you."

Carry a phrase book to help you along. People will warm up when you make an effort to speak their language.

If you won't get back before April 15th, you need to fill out a Federal Income tax extension form. By proving you were out of the country, you have an automatic 90-day extension (you can show a copy of your airline ticket). However, you must have enough paid into the IRS in order not to suffer penalties.

If someone is taking care of your house, or you are renting it out, you need to fill out a Power of Attorney form giving someone you trust the legal right to handle your personal affairs, such as eviction of destructive renters or those who bounce rent checks. Leave that person with extra funds to pay for emergency or unexpected bills.

Fill out a will and register it in probate court. Notify your benefactor. It costs less than $10.00 to register.

Make sure your insurance payments are in order. Car, house, bike and any other insured items must have up-to-date premiums paid.

Carry a travel handbook that gives you the ins and outs of each country and major cities. Carry a Youth Hostel book with locations and phone numbers.

Today, with smart phones, you enjoy 24/7 connections to the world. However, you may need mail at some point.

Leave a travel itinerary with loved ones of post office addresses in major cities. Tell them to address the envelope with your name, c/o Poste Restante, Central Post Office, City and Country. Poste Restante is the international word for general delivery. You can pick up your mail at a post office by showing your passport. Tell your friends to write to each address three weeks in advance of the tentative dates you have written down on your itinerary. If you're not sure where you will be and don't want to write all your friends each time with a possible new address, you can have your friends write to one address in the states at your best friend's or parent's house and have your mail forwarded from there. It's easier that way. I can tell you that letters are like Christmas gifts, and mean so much when you are a long way from home.

Another nice communication mode is 'hotmail' or 'gmail' on the computer. You can pick up email virtually around the world today. You dial up your personal code and you can write and read letters to and from your friends. Check with any carrier to get hooked up.

Create a FB account where you can write stories and exhibit pictures from your travels. You'll be amazed at the audience that follows you.

Carry the international dialing phone number of your local bicycle shop. If you suffer a major breakdown, they can express mail you a replacement. By keeping stocked with parts from the pack list, you should be covered.

When traveling through multiple countries, you must have a plane ticket home, and enough money to show you are financially responsible while touring that country. Otherwise, authorities may not let you enter their country.

Check with your travel agent to see if you need a visa for a particular country, or whether they give an automatic 30-day visa. Once you arrive in a country that has granted you an automatic visa, but you didn't obtain one for the next country you will visit--you can apply at the embassy in the capitol of the country you are now touring. Remember to take extra pictures.

Always be cordial and smile. Be as neat and clean as you can and act respectfully toward authorities.

For anyone going on a long-distance tour, buy a special padded seat cover with the latest in silicone cushioning. It will save your rear end. For double insurance, seats now offer this material and you can add the cover for ultimate comfort. I ride a Serfas Full Suspension Hybrid touring seat. It's around $45.00.

PHYSICAL CONDITIONING

Your physical preparation is one of the most important keys to enjoyment while on tour. Ride your bike every day for a month before departure. If you're headed into the mountains, find some steep grades where you live, and ride them with your loaded panniers. If none exist, ride a high resistance stationary bike at the local health club.

If you fail to prepare your legs, a slight strain or ligament pull will finish you abruptly on a bicycle adventure because it will get worse with every added mile. Make sure you avoid that: get into pedaling shape.

BIKE SECURITY

Your bike security at night or while visiting a monument is important. Either check into a safe hotel where you can keep the bike in your room (I cable it to a pipe or anything secure), or have someone in your party stay with the cycles and gear. Lock the bikes to something solid and keep equipment in your tent at night.

One point on safety: cut a fiberglass bicycle safety flagpole to three feet. Push it through the bungee cords on the rear of your pack so that it sticks two feet out to the traffic side in whatever country you're touring. This technique keeps drivers from scaring the heck out of you because it forces them to pass at a safer distance, or wait to pass at a better time. For added safety, I fly another orange flag, hose clamped to the rear rack, eight feet up vertically.

ATTITUDE

Patience: In developing world countries, during any situation, remain calm, patient and respectful. Learn to accept their ways, even though they may be frustrating, and different from your own.

One last point on international bicycle touring—you are pedaling into strange lands, meeting new people and experiencing different cultures. You will have the time of your life. Leave excess baggage like prejudice, discrimination and discourtesy at home. Stretch your emotional, mental and spiritual wings to learn about the world. Ride as a personal ambassador from your country. The impressions you make on people will remain with them forever. Share a smile, kind words and good things will come your way.

Enjoy a grand bicycle adventure in good health and high spirits.

WHAT TO TAKE AND HOW TO PACK IT

One of the most frustrating feelings on a bicycle tour is when you dig into your pack for something and can't find it. Even worse is realizing you didn't bring it. It can be as small as a pair of tweezers or as important as a spoke wrench. The best way to prevent such a calamity is to keep a pack list that you can check off before leaving for your adventure.

Special precautions must be taken in five areas each time you load your gear into your panniers. When you need an item, you want it easily available. That goes double for your first aid kit.

International tours require extra attention to details, and at least three months advance preparation.

EQUIPMENT ORGANIZATION

Organizing your equipment is the best way to have it ready for your use. If it's small, light and you use it often, the best storage place is a zipper pouch on the rear panniers or your daypack. Depending on how you stand your bike, items used often need to be on the free side of the bike. For efficiency, group common items like a toothbrush and soap in the same nylon 'ditty' bags. These drawstring pouches are handy. You can use clear plastic bags to separate clothes into organized compartments. You can do the same for tire repair tools.

When your gear is packed, especially on your first trip, it takes a few days of rearranging everything to place it where you like. Once that's accomplished, draw a schematic of where everything is placed. Use it for quick reference when packing for future rides.

WEIGHT DISTRIBUTION

The first rule in bicycling touring is: If you don't need or use it, leave it. Why? Simple—weight adds up quickly. Every excess pound you pack will cost you in bike stability and miles covered daily. When riding with four panniers, you need to pack the heaviest equipment—like stove, fry pan, and cable lock—into the lowest sections of your rear panniers. That will keep your "lean" weight closer to the ground. Lean weight means the amount of weight you have on the bike and where it is located. If you pack heavy items higher up in the panniers, the bike will be top heavy.

When loading your bicycle, you need to balance weight from side to side. More weight should be in the rear panniers than in the front. If you experience a shimmy in your handlebars, it means you have too much in your handlebar bag. Keep less than four pounds in it. If a shimmy persists, lighten your front panniers and check the side to side balance. Traditional touring bikes with light frames and skinny tires have a shimmy problem more than touring mountain bikes. That's why I recommend a mountain bike for touring.

CAMERA EQUIPMENT CARE

Keep your camera equipment in plastic bags at all times. While on tour, dust swirls around you from cars and the wind. Also, you must be concerned about rain. Large zip lock freezer bags work well, and you can see through them and reuse them. Keep camera gear in the daypack cushioned over your sleeping bag and air mattress rolls.

DAYPACK AND INTERNAL FRAME BACKPACK

A small daypack will keep many of your valuables safe and ready for use. They are as handy as any book pack that you used back in school. It'll carry your camera and valuable gear that you want with you at a moment's notice.

A 2,000 to 3,000 cubic inch internal frame pack with three side compartments is an excellent addition to your versatility while on tour. You can store your air mattress, gear, along with extra digital cards, valuables and food. Make it the easy access pack to your most often used gear. If you happen to find yourself in a backpacking situation, you're ready to go.

RAINPROOFING YOUR GEAR

No doubt about it, you're at the mercy of the elements on a bicycle tour. Your equipment must be kept dry. Wrap everything each morning in plastic bags. Keep your rain suit available. Make certain your camera gear is rain proofed. Do the same for your sleeping bag and tent.

NIGHT LIGHT IN YOUR TENT

Miners lamps cost $20.00 and will give you ample light for writing in the tent or cooking dinner outside.

CYCLING SHOES, GLOVES, GLASSES, SHORTS AND HELMET

Buy the best, most comfortable cycling shoes you can afford. Do not ride with tennis shoes. You need the plastic or steel shank on the bottom of the shoes to give you protection from the pedals. Without that shank, you will be in a lot of pain and cause your legs to waste a lot of energy to compensate.

Buy a good pair of cycling gloves to protect you from pounding your hands to death. The first week of a cycling trip, keep shaking your hands at regular intervals so you won't crush the ulnar nerve in the palm of the hand. If you have 'aero' bars, you will be able to give your hands a rest. That bar will take the pressure off your ulnar nerve. I highly recommend it.

With the ozone vanishing, you need to buy 100% UV glasses to stop damage to your eyes. I wear the very best eye protection. I buy the sunglasses with leather side blocks to protect you from the wind and they have a cord to keep them around your neck.

Buy two pairs of cycling shorts, either regular touring shorts or Lycra. Make sure you buy the suede-padded shorts instead of leather because sued is easier to wash and wear. If you are riding in extremely sunny weather, you might want to wear thin Thermax protection in the form of a shirt that covers your arms and neck. If it's blistering sunshine, wear thin tights to protect your legs from hours of radiation from the sun. A tan looks nice, but the damage to your skin accumulates into wrinkles, and potential skin cancers. Your body does not need all that sun. Protect your face daily with maximum sun block.

Always wear a helmet. One person on average per day dies in the USA while riding a bicycle each year. Over 50,000 persons visit hospitals with broken bones and cuts bad enough to need medical attention after bike crashes each year. The most serious accidents are head injuries because people weren't wearing helmets. For touring, be certain to have a visor on your helmet for sun protection. They can stitch you up, and they can set your broken bones—but they can't pour your brains back into your head the right way. Wear a helmet. If the helmet doesn't have a visor, you can buy one at a motorcycle shop and drill new holes and fit it on yourself.

INTERNATIONAL TOURING

Any time you ride into a foreign country; you're subject to different conditions. You may be vulnerable to infectious diseases, tainted food and water. You need extra precautions with eating, drinking and medicine. Boil, use drops or filter your water, and eat only cooked foods. Always peel fruits and vegetables. You might consider becoming a temporary vegetarian once you see how dairy products and meats are left out in the sun with flies crawling everywhere.

Because you will not be able to bathe every day, carry an antifungal ointment. Take a washcloth and wipe yourself down nightly with water from your bottles. This will help prevent fungal growth on your skin. For poison ivy or other skin rashes, carry Micatin cream.

Your passport is vulnerable to theft. ALWAYS keep it and money on your person, in a pouch around your neck or in your pack. Your daypack should always go with you on a break, or have a trusted friend watch the gear while you go to the restroom.

During a tour in foreign countries, preventive maintenance is very important. Check your spokes often and take plenty of spare nuts and bolts. Two spare tubes and one extra tire are a minimum. Carry enough patch gear for 20 punctures. You will need a freewheel puller wrench, chain breaker and rear derailleur. In developing world countries, strongly consider a mountain bike converted for touring, i.e., put drop bars on it, 'aero' bars, and ride with 1.75 tires with a 40 spoke 26-inch rim. For heavily mountainous countries, try a 24 front 'Granny' gear chain ring to a 34 teeth rear freewheel or cassette climbing gear.

THE BIG ITEMS

Your tent, sleeping bag, daypack and air mattress are the bulky pieces that must balance over the rear axle. Strap your tent forward under the seat and your sleeping bag behind it. The air mattress will fit over the tent. A second set of crossed bungee cords will secure your daypack. Check for hanging straps or bungee cords—EVERY TIME you finish packing your bicycle. Otherwise, you will wrap them around the freewheel or spokes. The results can tear up your wheel alignment and worse.

FUEL BOTTLE AND GEAR PLACEMENT

You will find your own style for placing equipment. However, the fuel bottle is a potentially troublesome item. Some riders place it in their lower water bottle clip on the down tube. You can wrap it in plastic and set it upright in the rear pouch of your panniers. In either case, be certain to secure the opening from leakage. This pack list may be customized to suit you. Use or discard items as you need them for yourself.

PACKING LIST

TOP OF FRONT PANNIER RACK
1. Sleeping Bag and Silk Cocoon in Waterproof Stuff Sack
2. Grey Handlebar Bag
   a. Front of Bike White Light (3 AAA)
   b. Rear of Bike LED Red Warning Light (2 AAA)
   c. Chamois Cream
   d. Tire Pressure Gauge
   e. Riding Carb Fuel
   f. Eyeglass Cleaning Liquid & Cloth
   g. Sunglass Case W/Reg. Glasses
   h. SPF 100 Sun Block
   i. SPF 50 Chap Stick
   j. Hand Sanitizer

    k. Swiss Army Knife

    l. Mobile Phone

    m. Camera, extra digital cards

    n. Travel Wallet

LEFT FRONT PANNIERS ('B')

1. Instant Oatmeal
2. Hot Drink Mixes (tea, coffee, hot chocolate)
3. Peanut Butter
4. Bread or Tortillas
5. Three One-Gallon Freezer Bags
6. Three One-Quart Freezer Bags
7. Three One-Pint Freezer Bags
8. Riding Carb Fuel (Dried Fruit, Apples, Bananas, Oranges)
9. Stuff Sack with Energy Bars
10. Sports Drink Mix

RIGHT FRONT PANNIER ('A')

1. Spice Shaker
2. Vegetable Broth Cubes
3. Dinner Staples (Pasta, Lentils, Couscous, Quinoa, Etc.)
4. Dehydrated Evening Meals
5. Salad Fixings
6. Extra Riding Carb Fuel (Dried Fruit, Apples, Bananas, Oranges)

RIGHT REAR PANNIER ('D')

1. Outside Pocket
    a. First Aid Kit
    b. Folding Water Container
2. 0.6L Fuel Bottle in Freezer Bag
3. 325mL Fuel Bottle W/Pump
4. MSR 2.0 L Pot w/Strainer Lid
    a. Brunton Cook Stove
    b. Dish Towel
    c. Matches
    d. Pot Gripper

e. Fork

f. Liquid Soap

g. Scouring Pad

5. Snow Peak Individual Cook Set, MSR cook set, you decide for your needs

a. 0.8 L Cooking Pot

b. Lid

c. 10 oz. Cup

6. Gallon Freezer Bag

a. Plate

b. Long Handled Spoon

c. Long Handled Knife

d. Stove Wind Shield

7. Repair Kit

a. Assorted Bandages

b. 2 Tire Irons

c. Open End Wrenches, 7-10 Mm

d. Allen Wrenches, All Sizes to Fit Bike

e. Leatherman Squirt Pliers

f. 6" Adjustable Wrench

g. Chain Tool

h. Three Grease Rags

i. Nuts, Bolts (Assorted)

j. Chain Links

k. One Tire Patch Kit (6-8 Patches)

l. Brake Cable

m. Gear Cable

n. Brake Blocks

o. 4 – 6" Plastic Tie Straps

p. Short Length Elect. Tape

q. 26 X 1.5 – 1.75 Presta Valve Tube

r. Tent Seam Sealer

LEFT REAR PANNIER ('C')

1. Outside Pocket

a. Clothes Drying Net Bag

    b. Insect Repellent
    c. Cable and Combination Lock
    d. Chain Lube, Grease Rag & Small Tube of Grease Remover Hand Cleaner in Plastic Bag

2. Street Clothes Stuff Sack
    a. 1 – PR. Lt. Wt. Long Pants w/zippered Legs
    b. 1 – Lt. Wt. Long Sleeve Shirt w/roll up sleeves
    c. 1 – Pr. Lt. Wt. Underwear
    d. 1 – T Shirt
    e. 1 - Swim Suit

3. Bike Wear Stuff Sack
    a. 1 – Pr. Biking Socks
    b. 1 - Thermax Long Sleeve Jersey
    c. 1 - Thin Sun Protection Long Sleeve Jersey
    d. 1 – Pr. Riding Shorts
    e. 1 – Pr. Biking Tights

4. Cold Weather Stuff Sack
    a. 1 - Under Armor Top
    b. 1 - Under Armor Bottom
    c. 1- Stocking Cap

5. Shower Sandals in Net Bag

6. Toiletry Kit
    a. 30 Days Flaxseed
    b. 30 Days Aspirin
    c. 30 Days Glucosamine W/MSM
    d. 30 Days One-A-Day Vitamin
    e. Sewing Kit
    f. Gore-Tex Repair Kit
    g. Disposable razors
    h. Toothpaste
    i. Toothbrush
    j. Dental Floss
    k. Comb
    l. Travel Wallet Contents List

7. Small Net Bag
    a. Microfiber Towel

      b. Deodorant Bar Soap in plastic bag

TOP OF REAR PANNIER RACK

1. Duffle Bag, preferably oblong and squared off
    a. Rain Protection Plastic Bag W/Closure Device
    b. Tent in Stuff Sack
    c. Poles in Stuff Sack
    d. Ground Cloth & Rain Fly in Stuff Sack
    e. 14 Tent Stakes in Bag (1 Extra)
    f. Air Mattress in Stuff Sack
    g. Lightweight Camping Chair
    h. Plastic Bag for Bicycle Seat Rain Cover
    i. 30' Of Nylon Cord
    j. Mini Clothes Pins

2. Red & Black Daypack
    a. Rain Cover Plastic Bag W/Velcro Strap Closure
    b. Rain Jacket
    c. Rain Gear Stuff Sack
        i. Rain Pants
        ii. Rain Booties
        iii. Helmet Cover
        iv. Gloves
    d. Gallon Plastic Freezer Bag
        i. Gear Location Schematic
        ii. Maps
        iii. Bike Specs.
    e. Zippered Pocket
        i. Night LED Head Light (3 AAA)
        ii. Ear Plugs
        iii. SPF 50 Chap Stick
        iv. Nighttime Eye Cover
        v. Spare Batteries
            1. 3 - AAA
            2. Camera
    f. One Roll Camper Toilet Paper in Plastic Bag
    g. Small Net Bag
        i. Phone Charger

   ii. Camera Battery Charger

  h. Quart Freezer Bag

   i. Postcard Stamps

   ii. Journal

   iii. Address List

 i. Two Pens

 j. Two carabineers on Outside of pack

 k. Water purification tablets

 l. Cell phone

 m. Lap top computer

REMOVABLE BIKE ACCESSORIES

1. Frame Mounted Air Pump
2. 3 Water Bottles
3. Handlebar Mount Warning Bell
4. Rear View Mirror
5. Two 14" Bungee Cords
6. Four 20" Bungee Cords
7. One 11" Bungee Cord
8. One Short 27" Safety Flag
9. One Long 6' Safety Flag
10. Two Parking Brake 11" Velcro Straps
11. Bike Computer(1 Cr 2032 + 1 12v)
12. 3 Spokes with Nipples Mounted on Left Chain Stay
13. Two Extra Halo Sweat Bands on Aero Bars

WEARING TO RIDE

1. Helmet
2. Halo Sweat Band
3. Sunglasses
4. Short Sleeve Bike Jersey
5. Bike Shorts
6. Bike Socks
7. Bike Shoes
8. Bike Gloves
9. Riding Food in Jersey Pockets

10. Hydration Pack

NEEDED (make yourself a 'need to buy' list)

1. **Long Handled Peanut butter Spreading Knife 8" REI Campware Knife**
2. Adjustable nylon webbing straps instead of bungee cords
3. Better Velcro straps to attach grey handlebar bag to sleeping bag and front pannier rack
4. Ink marker for tire tube to mark leak

On departure day pack added

1. Lip Balm
2. Bike Repair Book
3. Camera Instructions
4. Destination Tour Book
5. Blanket & Pillow
6. Toiletry Kit
7. Sunglass Case W/Sunglasses
8. Eye Cover for Sleeping
9. Riding Clothes
10. Riding Shoes
11. Bike Computer
12. Radio w/earphone

On Departure Day Pack (again, use as backup)

1. One Roll Toilet Paper
2. Trowel
3. Packable Broad Brim Hat

Travel Clothing

1. Long Pants
2. Long Sleeve Shirt
3. North Face Shoes
4. Normal Socks
5. Poly Underwear
6. Prescription Glasses

Ship Back – UPS (You may want to ship gear back to lighten load, example)

1. North Face Shoes
2. Normal Socks
3. 2 Duffel Bags
4. Blanket and Pillow
5. Eye Cover for Sleeping
6. Radio w/earphone
7. Tool Kit stuff
    a. Straight Blade Screwdriver
    b. Side Cutters

MAIL BACK ON LEAVING DESTINATION CITY OR COUNTRY

1. Tour Book
2. Bike Repair Book
3. Camera Instruction

First Aid Kit

- 6 -10 4x4" Pads for Cleaning Wound and Soaking Blood
- 4 - 6 4x4" <u>Non-Stick</u> Pads for Covering Wound
- 1 – 2" Ace Stretch Wrap
- 1 Triangular Arm Sling
- 4-8 Large Safety Pins
- 4-6 Bandage Strips With 2 To 3 Inch Square Pads
- Tape, 1 Inch Wide, Surgical Tape (3-6 Yards or Meters).
- 6-10 Packets Or 1 Small 2-3 Oz. Bottle of Wound Sanitizer/ Cleaner Betadine, Hibiclens, Peroxide, Baby Wipes or Soap and Water
- 1 Small Tube Triple Antibiotic Salve for Dressing Cuts and Abrasions
- 1 Small Tube, Hydrocortisone, 1% Or 2.5%,Topical Usage Only. Reduces Inflammation, Rashes, Saddle Sores and Allergic Reactions.
- 10-20 Tablets/Capsules Tylenol, *Acetaminophen*: For Muscle and Body Pain, Joint Pain, Headaches, Fever, Allergies, Cough, Cold, And Flu

- 10-20 Tablets/Capsules Motrin Or Advil, *Ibuprofen*: Anti-Inflammatory, Pain Killer
    - 5-10 Tablets/Capsules Benadryl, *Diphenhydramine Hydrochloride*: General Anesthetic, Antihistamine, Anti Swelling, Sleeping Pill, Sedative, Anti Bleeding - Called: Nuprin, Medipren, Brufen, Anti-Vomiting/Nausea, Motion Sickness
- 3-4 Band Aids ½" Wide (1.5 Cm & 2.5 Cm Wide),Keep Some in Tool Kit, In Small Plastic Bag
- 3-4 Band Aids 1" Wide (1.5 Cm & 2.5 Cm Wide),Keep Some in Tool Kit, In Small Plastic Bag
- Moleskin- Prevent Blister
- Molefoam – Protect Blister
- Solarcaine -Sunburn Relief
- Imodium Ad- Anti-Diarrheal
- Visine - Eye Irritation
- Eucerine - Moisturizing Lotion
- Rolaids - Anti-Acid
- Lotromin Af - Anti Fungal
- Calamine - Sting / Itch Relief

Safety and extras for national and international travel

1. Take a six-foot, fiberglass orange/lime green flagpole, lock to back rack.
2. Take a three-foot, fiberglass orange/lime green traffic side flagpole, bungee into traffic side.
3. Two extra tires, two extra tubes, 20 patches.
4. One extra chain.
5. Extra rear derailleur.
6. Extra freewheel or rear cassette.
7. Passport, shot records, international driver's license, Scuba Diving Card, extra passport sized pictures, hostel card, silk sheet for sleeping bag, bird book, Frisbee (optional), Hacky sack, snake bite kit, 30 feet of nylon cord, spare toe clip, extra nuts, washers and bolts, toe clip strap, swimmer's goggles, malaria pills, small binoculars, metric conversion card, bear repellant spray.

8. When traveling on a train, boat or plane, make sure you buy a NEW fuel bottle and mark it a 'water' bottle with duct tape. If the TSA people try to confiscate it, and they will, put some water in it and drink it to show them. Otherwise, they will take it away from you, and you will be without a fuel bottle when you reach South America or Africa or some other place.

9. Spare brake cable, spare gearing cable, spare brake pads, spare pulley, photocopies of passport, driver's license, sewing kit, MSR stove cleaner and repair kit, birth certificate copy, water purification tablets, suture and thread, folding gallon container, spare spokes front and back, spare reading glasses, chain oil, chain breaker, freewheel cog remover, spare ball bearings, bottom bracket puller, pocket vice, crank remover, crazy glue, valve stem remover, swimsuit, cable and combination lock.

INTERNATIONAL TOURING RECOMMENDATIONS

When riding outside the grocery-store-and-fast-food borders of the United States, you open yourself up to new culinary challenges and dangers. In America, you can count on clean water. The U.S. Department of Agriculture inspects meats. Most people speak English. You enjoy smooth roads and easy living.

You're sick of it, right? Too many motor home mentalities! Cable TV hookups in campsites! Every town in America looks like every other town. First you see the Golden Arches, followed by Wendy's, Subway, Arby's and Pizza Hut. Everyone walking out of a fast-food restaurant looks like they need special coaching from Jenny Craig and the TV program: Biggest Losers! Ye gads! Whatever happened to regional flavor, small town diners, personal dress and style? Does anyone remember what an old-time hardware store smells like? Do they know the wooden floors creak? Not a chance!

Sounds like you're ready to see how the other 95 percent lives. Hold onto your handlebars and pull up your Lycra shorts because you're in for one heck of a surprise. You face amazing sights and experiences in the developing world.

Always be aware of your potential circumstances on tour in developing countries. Be smart! Be prudent! Be prepared! Your life may depend on your thoughtful and measured actions. You cannot hope someone will rescue you like they do in the movies.

Anytime you ride into a foreign country, you're subject to conditions you won't find at home. You may be vulnerable to infectious diseases, tainted food and contaminated water. You need extra precautions with eating, drinking and medicine.

RIDING OUTSIDE THE UNITED STATES

While on tour in any one of more than 190 countries, give or take a revolution every five years, you will notice many differences. The freedoms you take for granted at home may be turned upside down in other countries. The way people dress on the altiplano, treeless land above 12,000 feet in Bolivia, is different from the natives in Bali. People in the Middle East bow to Allah five times a day and the women are covered except for their eyes. Australia's kangaroos may enthrall you with their 40-foot leaps. Europe's architecture and history will seduce you. The cultures, languages, animals and people you visit will change dramatically from country to country. Your patience and understanding will be challenged often in foreign lands.

Please enjoy that people around the world offer smiles and friendships. They laugh, cry and struggle through different parts of their lives, just like you do. You travel through the 'village' of humanity.

Along the way, you need to adapt. That 'adaptation' keys your success. When it comes to eating, you face challenges and fabulous experiences.

First, you face a 90 percent certainty of suffering from food poisoning or bacterial disruption of your stomach and colon. Whether it's giardia cysts, worms, dysentery, hepatitis or food poisoning—you're headed for the bathroom. The key: accept its inevitability, treat it, endure it and get on with your tour. Take along medicine for diarrhea and pills to kill parasites. Obtain those medications in your doctor's office.

WATER ON INTERNATIONAL TOURS

The primary concern on international tours: water! The rule remains simple:

- Always filter your water.
- Use purification tablets to ensure safety.

Make certain when you're filtering water to avoid mixing droplets of unfiltered water with filtered water. Just one unfiltered or untreated droplet can cause you sickness. That's why a purification tablet gives you a second line of defense in making your water safe.

No matter how much time it takes to filter water, do it painstakingly. It can mean the difference between miles of smiles and days of lying on your back with giardia making your colon feel like it's an arena for a bumper-car rally.

DISEASES

Several diseases await you while on tour in developing countries. Be prudent and you will save yourself from most of them. Take every preventative shot in the book to protect yourself. Your physician can provide immunizations for you.

Hepatitis causes one heck of a lot of misery in developing countries. To combat it, take gamma-globulin shots that last up to six months. So far, so good! Make sure you take the shot several weeks before the trip, and avoid taking a gamma-globulin shot with any live virus vaccines. Your doctor will know about that.

If you contract hepatitis, you will feel like someone used your body as a practice target for a bow and arrow. You will be weak, your eyes will turn yellow, and your urine will darken.

You can contract hepatitis from food or water. If you come down with it, see a doctor as quickly as possible.

The Inca Two-Step, or Montezuma's Revenge, or Buddha's Belly give you an idea of 'bowel affliction' called diarrhea in the United States. You will spend entire days on the toilet and your face in the lavatory! If you discover blood in your feces, along with cramps in your stomach, it could be dysentery. You may need to take tetracycline. See a doctor.

Upon returning from any international tour, have your feces, blood and urine checked for bugs.

FOOD TRANSPORT OVER LONG DISTANCES

One of your biggest challenges will be transporting food and water across long stretches of desert or uninhabited mountains. Be sure to look at a map and find out how far it is to the next food and water. We have carried as much as six days of food with us when we rode from La Paz, Bolivia to Arica, Chile. Our bikes looked more like pack mules than touring machines.

Our supplies included 10 days' worth of oatmeal, dried beans and rice, dried breads and rolls, tuna, dried fruit, potatoes, carrots and onions, and other sturdy, non-perishable foods. With rice and beans, and oatmeal—you can enjoy protein and carbs to power you anywhere.

In desert situations, like the Atacama Desert of Chile, or the Sahara in Africa, you're looking at hundreds of miles of sand. You won't see a fly or mosquito. You will need to bring four gallons of water with you to ensure making it to the next roadhouse. That's especially important on the Nullarbor Plains (treeless) in the Outback of Australia, where temperatures exceed 120 degrees Fahrenheit and higher. The sun sucks water out of your skin like a wet-vac vacuum. I've toured 100 miles in Death Valley at 116 degrees F, 190 degrees at ground level. I have downed five gallons in one day, and never hit the bathroom!

PREVENTATIVE MAINTENANCE AND HEALTH ON TOUR

Because you will not be able to bathe every day, carry antifungal ointment. Or, take a 1.5 gallon 'shower bag' with you offered at most camping stores. You can rinse down, soap up, and rinse off within three minutes. Just hang the bag on a tree and, voila, you're clean for sleeping.

Great invention! Still carry the anti-fungal ointment! Also carry cortisone cream for poison ivy.

During a tour anywhere, preventative maintenance: very important! Check your spokes and screws daily to make sure they are tight. Gear ratio: 24 to a 34-rear granny! No need to bust your guts when you can spin with ease!

There's a reason you're traveling along adventure highway. As John Muir wrote, "Camp out among the grass and gentians of glacier meadows, in craggy garden nooks full of Nature's darlings. Climb the mountains and get their good tidings. Nature's peace will flow into you as sunshine flows into trees. The winds will blow their freshness into you, and the storms their energy, while cares will drop off like autumn leaves."

Be smart. Stay prepared. Enjoy the peace and silence. It's all good!

BAKER'S DOZEN SUGGESTIONS

You will develop dozens of personal habits while touring. Your gear will be placed where you want it and you will evolve an almost ritualistic style of doing things.

Of course, the most important think you can do is buy a good bike and have a touring veteran fit it to your body. Have the bike fitted at four junctures:

- Fit the right-sized bike for your height.
- Fit your seat to pedal height. With your shoe heel at 6:00 o'clock position while sitting in the seat, have someone hold you straight, you need to have a 10 percent bend in the knee. This will give you maximum pedal, muscle and power coordination.
- Fit your knee to your pedal axle. You should be able to drop a plumb line straight from the back of your patella to the axle of the pedal. Pedal will be located at 9 o'clock position on the left side of the bike. Adjust your seat to make sure you're exactly in line with your patella and the axle for a perfect fit and comfort.
- Fit the length from your seat to your handlebars. A general rule of thumb is to place your elbow at the tip of the seat and your longest

middle finger will touch the handlebars for a perfect riding angle and fit. Go to a professional bike shop to get it done for you if you are unsure.

Buy a bike from a good bicycle store where you will enjoy good service after the sale. If you buy mail order, be sure you know what you're doing or have a friend who knows what he or she is doing to help you select the best bike.

Here's that Baker's Dozen ideas:

- No matter how much you ride, someday you will take a fall. Since you don't know how bad the fall will be, you must anticipate the worst and wear a helmet. About 2.5 Americans die daily from falling off bicycles. That's 900 a year. Most of them cracked their heads like an egg yolk and didn't live. About 50,000 suffer broken bones, cuts and other injuries. Wear your helmet so you don't become a statistic. Buy and ANSI approved helmet and strap it on every time you get on your bicycle!

- Buy the best sunglasses you can afford to protect your eyes. Protect yourself from deadly radiation from constant sun burning down on your face and body by covering your body with long sleeve jerseys and tights.

- Buy an excellent pair of shoes designed specifically for bicycle riding with steel or plastic shank along the foot bed to give your even pressure and comfort. Without a good shoe, your food will feel more pressure pain than you can imagine. Check www.performancebike.com ; www.bikenashbar.com ; www.REI.com .

- Learn how to maintain and repair your bicycle. Take a bicycle repair class with hands-on instruction. You need to be able to take apart your head tube, hubs, bottom bracket and freewheel or cassette assembly. If you're on a world tour, you need to be able to true your wheels and possibly rebuild a rim! You must know how to repair a tube or save a tire with 'duct tape' to the side walls to get more mileage when you're in a remote village in South America. Take the tools you need and know how to use them.

- Your nutrition on a bike trip is important. Stay as close to high carbohydrates and simple proteins as possible for maximum efficiency. You will gain more stamina, power and endurance from pasta, grains, fruits, cereals, vegetables and breads. You may want to take multiple vitamins on an extended tour for 'added' nutrition. Your body suffers considerable depletion of resources while pedaling days on end.

- Also, in order to defend against skin cancer, cover your body with long sleeve jersey and tights and hood down from your helmet to protect your ears and neck. Use 50 block sunscreen and lip balm.

- Drink liquids constantly. Water provides the best drink on tour.

- While touring in high mountains, allow your body to acclimate itself to the altitude. If not, you could suffer from altitude sickness. If you push too hard, too fast, you could suffer from pulmonary edema. If you feel weak, short of breath and start coughing, drop below 10,000 feet and stay there for a few days until you feel well enough to climb again. Cerebral edema is a more serious sickness because it affects your brain. You will suffer a pounding headache and possible double vision. If you do not take action, death could result. Descend to below 10,000 feet and get medical attention.

- When taking airlines and trains to major destinations, you will have to box your bike for transport. Visit a bicycle shop and pick out a box that fits your bike, or ask them to save you one, or check out their dumpster for extra boxes. Learn how to break your bike down and put it back together so you won't depend on a bike shop.

- You will attract lots of attention while touring and many people will invite you into their homes. I have never encountered a problem, but you need to be cautious, especially if you are a woman. You might accept lodging only if you meet a family or couple. I would shy away from single men asking you over to stay the night. Also, many men enjoy a faster cadence and move ahead of their women partners. This is important: if you're on tour with your wife or a female companion, ride behind her so you stay together. If you pedal too far ahead, she will feel alone and vulnerable. She will be highly agitated given enough time, and your relationship will suffer—along with your tour. Trust me on this one, guys!

- Dogs can be the bane of your bicycling tour. They will frighten the daylights out of you and worse, bite you. You could be sent to the hospital for stitches or rabies shots. If a dog or dogs attack, they usually bark first, so you know they are coming. It's worth your efforts to deal with their attacks quickly. Always be alert for dogs by keeping an eye on a house or any areas you think houses dogs. If you can outrun dogs by pedaling past their territory, go for it. You can carry a dog repellant spray, or better yet, pull your traffic side three-foot-long fiberglass safety pole out from under your bungee cords and show it to them by waving it back and forth. That 'whip' will calm them down quickly and they will leave you alone. If pressed, carry a few stones in your handlebar bag and throw them at the dogs. Carry wasp & hornet spray in a can with a 30-foot stream. Aim at their faces. As a last resort, dismount your bike and walk behind it as you move out of their territory.
- Always be prepared for survival situations by carrying ample water, food and shelter. Carry minimum amounts of food that will keep you fed for up to seven days in remote regions. Make sure you can stay warm in a summer blizzard at high altitude. Bring those waterproof glove protectors and rain booties to keep hands and feet dry and warm.
- Leave the road and find camp 1.5 to 2.0 hours before dusk. If you happen to get caught in the dark, attach a front LED headlight and rear blinking LED red light. You can carry a blinking strobe light to let traffic know your presence.

BREAKING DOWN AND PACKING YOUR BIKE FOR TRAVEL

Secure the right sized box for your bike. You can buy a plastic box at bike shops if you plan to have a safe place at your destination to store it. If not, a cardboard box will work fine.

Break down your bike by taking off the handlebars, front wheel, pedals, seat and pulling off the rear derailleur. Take the rear derailleur off the dropout, tape it to the chain and encase it in cloth with tape. Do not forget this procedure or you may suffer a bent dropout hanger and possibly a broken rear derailleur. Lock the front forks with a plastic axle and secure it with tape. That will stabilize the forks from breakage. Secure all nuts and bolts and pack the bike with paper so it won't move inside the box. Place the front rack under the forks. The front wheel will fit beside the frame opposite the chain drive side. Tape the pedals to the frame so as not to lose them along with the bike seat and shaft. Slip a piece of cardboard between the wheel and your bike so it won't suffer scratches. Everything you can do to keep the bike locked solidly still in the box is important. Toss in your six-foot fiberglass safety flag and three-foot fiberglass traffic-side safety flag along with empty water bottles. Tape it up with plastic tape. Tape all the four corners, and all seams for extra strength on international journeys where they throw your gear around without regard to damage to your precious bike.

BEST SAFETY GEAR ON THE PLANET FOR CYCLISTS

Let's cover the most important safety device on your bike: be sure to strap that six-foot-long fiberglass pole with orange/lime green and even white safety flag to your rear rack. A second three-foot fiberglass safety pole with orange/lime green flag will fit under your bungee cords that secure your rear pack to the rack—about 18 inches into traffic. In town, you can shove it closer to the bike, so you won't be such a 'wide' profile trying to maneuver around cars in heavy traffic.

The total affect is two orange, flapping flags that can be seen a half-mile away. They get the attention of approaching drivers both front and rear. When you garner their attention, you are less likely to suffer consequences. You must remember that you are sharing the road with at least 2,000 pounds of steel traveling at 65 miles per hour. Just one yawn or sneeze, a glance back at the kids, or a daydream could have a car running up the back of your panniers. Those flags are your lifeline to safety. Engage them as if your life depended on them. Buy at bike shop, K-Mart, Walmart or Target.

Finally, remember you are pedaling down adventure highway. You're an ambassador for your state or country. What you do affects others. Things you say or do last a lifetime to those you encounter. Make your tour a positive experience for all you meet. You will be rewarded with magical moments that last a lifetime in your heart and mind.

Chapter 30

CAMPING TECHNIQUES, BEAR AND MOUNTAIN LION SAFETY, SAFE WATER, PERSONAL HYGIENE, COOKING, CLEANING, HUMAN WASTE, LEAVE NO TRACE, WILDERNESS SURVIVAL

"To many Americans, the wilderness is little more than a retreat from the tensions of civilization. To others, it is a testing place—a vanishing frontier where humans can rediscover basic values. And to a few, the wilderness is nothing less than an almost holy source of self-renewal. But for every man, woman and child, the ultimate lesson that nature teaches is simply this: man's fate is inextricably linked to that of the world at large, and to all of the other creatures that live upon it." Unknown

Every time you step into the wilderness, it provides you with uncommon splendor and beauty. What can you do to preserve it? Answer: "Leave No Trace!"

By following the established protocol in this chapter whether you ride a bicycle, backpack, climb mountains, fish, raft, canoe, hike, sail or any other wilderness activity—take only photographs and leave only footprints.

For sure, my dad always told me, "Son, when you go camping, always leave the place nicer than you found it."

To this day, I have picked up a half million pieces of trash in my life, if not more. I volunteer to pick up rivers, roadways, campgrounds, mountain paths and any place I see trash. Yes, it's frustrating that many careless outdoor people toss their cans, bottles and glass containers without a blink. I also advocate for a 10-cent deposit/return law like Michigan's to stop the incredible littering of the landscape. It drives me crazy that billions of humans take no responsibility for their landscape around the planet.

Nonetheless, all of us enjoy a stake in our world's well-being and our own as we live this great life adventure. I hope you become one of the people that care and care deeply. This Chapter will show you how to preserve the wilderness.

Whether you hike, backpack, canoe, climb, bicycle or any other mode of adventuring—these techniques will guide you.

WILDERNESS CAMPING

CAMPING AND COOKING IN ESTABLISHED CAMPGROUNDS:

Making Camp
Cooking and Food Storage
Camping and Cooking in a Primitive Area
Make Camp in Primitive Areas
Building Campfires Safely in the Wilderness
Fire in Your Tent
Candle Lantern
Sanitation and Human Waste in the Wilderness
Cleaning and Hygiene
Bear and Lion Country
Rules for Camping in Bear and Lion Country
If a Bear or Mountain Lion Should Confront You

When adventuring—shelter and food take on a whole new significance, especially internationally. If you venture into developing world countries, being ill-prepared may cause you great discomfort. In the USA, it's not hard to find a camping park, motel, or bed and breakfast. You have many to choose from in every state and most of Canada.

In the developing world outside cities, lodging is next to impossible to find. That's why you must carry your own tent, sleeping bag and air mattress. For cooking meals, you need a stove, cookware, fuel, water and food supplies. When you're prepared with the basics, bicycle adventuring internationally will offer miles of smiles. Nothing beats a good night's sleep on a full stomach.

The most important gear a cyclist can carry is a top-quality tent. It must be big enough, light enough and waterproof. Quick "pitch time" is a nice extra. With so many tents on the market, how do you choose? You may have a friend who knows tents because he/she camps often. They have learned by experience. Have them go to the local camping outfitter with you to discuss the relative differences of tents. Buy good gear. You want to go cheap? Be my guest, but you will pay a terrible price in misery.

If you're on your own, a few tips may help in your purchase. For camping, your tent should be self-standing and six pounds or less. It should have a waterproof floor and sidewalls. Rip-stop nylon is your best bet for durability, or if you can afford it, buy a Gore-Tex fabric tent. Make sure the tent has a loop to hang clothes and candle lanterns from the ceiling. Make certain the tent is taut enough, so it won't flap in the wind. Get shock-corded poles for easier set up.

Make certain the rain fly covers the outside edges of the tent. Is your tent long enough? Can you sit up in it? Will you have room for two people and your gear? Is it warm enough for three seasons? A light color will be cooler in the summer and stand up under ultraviolet damaging rays better. Zippers should be YKK plastic. Make certain your tent features "No see 'em" netting. Check for good ventilation low in the tent you buy. Some manufacturers stand solidly behind their tents with excellent guarantees. Compare for a top choice. Purchase seam sealer and apply to the rain fly and corners of the tent, wherever the fabric has been sewn.

Once on the road, a few good habits will keep your tent in top condition for years of use. Purchase a nylon backed plastic tarp for a ground cloth. Cut it to fit 2" inside the outside boundary of your tent. This will help stop sharp objects from cutting your floor and it will keep out moisture.

You need to cut it 2" less all around the tent so it won't catch rainwater and pool it in the under you in the middle of the night.

Set up your tent every night as if it was going to rain. Find a high spot in the land and check for rocks and sticks before laying down the tarp. Never leave your tent out in the sun for extended lengths of time. Ultraviolet rays will damage the fabric. When taking down a tent, fold the poles and put them in a safe place immediately after you pull them out of their sleeves. This will prevent them from being stepped on. Count stakes each time you put your tent into the stuff sack. After a rain, either dry out the tent in the morning or at the earliest moment. For storage, make certain your tent is bone dry before putting it away for the winter.

After your tent, purchase a warm, comfortable sleeping bag. You have two choices: goose down or fiber fill. Having used both many times, it's this bicycle camper's opinion that for three season bicycling, a three-pound, 20-degree Fahrenheit, fiber fill mummy bag is your best bet. It dries easier and stands up to usage many years longer. Down shifts and leaves cold spots after a time and the loft breaks down. However, you may have a friend who swears by down for its compact ability and lighter weight. It becomes a personal decision.

No matter what your choice, buy a quality mummy bag from a reputable company. Make certain it's long enough and features a contoured hood enclosure with a draw string so all that is not covered when it's cold is your mouth. Make certain your bag is designed so the baffle flap drapes DOWN over the zipper from the inside. Gravity will keep that baffle covering the entire length of the zipper and stop any cold air from entering your bag. Expect to pay more for a down bag.

Keep it in a waterproof bag and stuff sack when riding. If you forget, you will be sliding your bare body into a cold, wet bag one nightstand wonder why you didn't pay attention to these suggestions. Don't laugh, I have slept in wet, cold bags before.

No matter how good your tent and sleeping bag, misery stalks the bicyclist that fails to sleep on an air mattress. The best self-inflating air mattress on the market for cycling is a 3/4 length, 1" thick Thermo-Rest mattress by Cascade Designs. Buy a stuff sack to go with it. It's the best investment for comfort in the world.

While camping you need cookware. A copper-bottomed stainless-steel set with two pots, plastic cups is light and handy. Keep a scrubber and soap in the pot. A plastic fork and spoon are light. If you're traveling in a first world country, go with a propane gas stove, carry two extras. For overseas touring, go with an MSR International stove that burns any kind of fuel. Your Swiss Army knife is a vital part of your cooking utensils, along with a carrot/potato peeler. Add a small plastic cutting board. Always wash cookware after dinner, especially in the wilds. You don't want a grizzly sniffing your toes in the middle of the night.

Depending on how loaded you are, and the length of your adventure, a sleeping bag, tent and mattress will set on your back rack. You may have a front rack with a platform perfect for a sleeping bag. You need a bigger bike to fit this style of packing. Be sure to carry plastic bags to waterproof your sleeping bag. It wouldn't hurt to do the same for your tent and mattress.

The one thing you cannot count on during an adventure is a campground. Well before you begin looking, about 1 1/2 hour before dark, have water bottles filled and an extra full gallon. If the water quality is questionable, purify by tablets, drops or filtration. Purchase your food in advance. Such things as toilet paper, matches and stove fuel should be secured.

If you find a campground with showers and you're willing to pay the price, go for it. Try to keep away from dogs and loud music.

Often, you are nowhere near an organized campground, or in the case of Developing world, no such thing exists. You're on your own. That's a plus, because it offers you a chance to experience nature, animals and solitude.

The best way to find a campsite is to look for a dirt road that leads into the bush, trees, rocks, or out of sight of the road. If you can find a place near a river, lake or stream, so much the better (Please bathe with biodegradable soap). When you find a suitable spot, away from traffic, pitch your tent, EVERY TIME, as if it were going to rain. Exceptions are the Sahara Desert. I have broken my own rules a few times and it cost me dearly with ruined camera and miserable nights floating around in my tent, or trying to dodge the wet spots creeping up on my body as the bag absorbed more water. Pitch your tent on high ground. Check for rocks, twigs and roots before laying down the ground tarp. Set the front door away from the wind and possible rain. This will give you a wind break for cooking too. Make certain all stakes are secured and the rain fly is taut. Be sure to keep the ground cloth under the tent. Once the tent is secured, take the gear off your bike and put it into your tent. Cable lock your bike to a tree including both wheels. A combination lock will allow everyone in your party to use the same lock without using a key.

CAMPING AND COOKING IN ESTABLISHED CAMPGROUNDS

When camp in an established campground, many obstacles are overcome immediately. You enjoy a picnic table, water, washing facilities and seating area at your command. Nonetheless, you need to buy food and load up on water two to three hours before sunset in case you don't reach and established campground. Always check your map for locations.

MAKING CAMP

After finding a spot in a campground—one to two hours before dark—you can:

- Pitch your tent on high ground.
- Roll out the sleeping mattress and sleeping bag.
- Place all your gear in the tent. Always put your gear in the same places, so you know where to find specific items, even in the dark. Always place your flashlight or miner's lamp exactly in the same place so you can grab it when you need it.
- Make sure your 'miner's lamp' is on your head and ready to work as darkness falls. These LED headlamps can be purchased at camping outlets. You may look like a coal miner walking around in the dark, but you will find it very useful.
- Remember NOT to place any food in your tent, especially in bear country. Rule: cook and eat 100 yards from your tent, and then, hang food 100 yards from your tent. That means you may have to eat first, then, cook and eat food, and then, hang food in trees 100 yards from final camp site. Don't believe me? Think

you can get away with it? So did I! But when you wake up during the night with a grizzly or black bear pummeling you inside your tent or looking at you when you open the flaps—don't say I didn't warn you! In bear country, always carry bear spray with you from www.REI.com and other camping stores. It could save your life. I guarantee that you will be scared enough to wet your pants, but you could live!

- If you are not in bear country, you 'can' leave food in your tent as long as you remain in the tent. If you leave, or you have food odor in your tent, little critters will eat their way through the nylon and ruin your tent.
- Lock your bike to a tree or to your helmet inside your tent (if there are no trees or something to cable the bike). To do this, run the cable through the bike frame, then into your tent and lock it to your helmet strap. When you zip up the tent, the cable acts like an umbilical cord between it and your bike. If someone tries to make off with your bike, they won't get far before you notice half your tent being pulled away.
- Always light the match before turning on your gas burner. Never turn the gas on first, unless you want to make like a Saturn rocket and blast yourself to the moon.
- Set up your food and fixings, cutting board, utensils, pans, water bottles and spices.
- Prepare your meal.
- Enjoy!
- Wash, clean, dry all your pots and utensils. Replace and secure.
- Secure food in tree or bear box, or if you're looking for an exciting night of terror, leave it in your tent!

COOKING AND FOOD STORAGE

Before cooking your meal, make good use of the stove burner for heating water for tea or hot chocolate. If you're cooking by a campfire, let the wood burn down so you get an even heat from the coals. You'll also have to tackle the problem of balancing pots on the coals.

Once you have prepared the food for cooking by chopping and cutting, place the food into the cooking pot. As your dinner progresses, keep any eye on the food to keep it from burning.

After dinner, wash everything with soap and rinse with water. Leave no food out for the animals. Keep extra food in a locked food box—a wooden or metal box used in some campgrounds where animals are a concern. If there are no food boxes, and you're in bear or mountain lion country, do not store food in your tent. Hang your food in a tree 300 feet from your camp.

Leave none of your gear out in the rain. Either store it in the tent or under the tent vestibule.

CAMPING AND COOKING IN A PRIMITIVE AREA

Camping in primitive (wilderness) areas presents several challenges that must be considered. You must be more responsible to your environment, i.e., disposal of human waste, water contamination and generated food and paper waste. You are more susceptible to bears, raccoons, squirrels and wild pigs charging into your camp looking for food. If it's a big old grizzly, he might be looking for you because he carries the latest copy of the Gourmet Bear in Search of a Bicyclist. Take precautions when camping in the wilds.

Again, make certain you have loaded up on extra water two to three hours before dusk. Or carry a filter that can purify water if there are ample places to fetch it—such as in the mountains or in lake regions.

Next, look for a campsite well off the road and hidden away from the sight of others. Not only is it a good idea to 'vanish' into the wilderness for personal safety, you will sleep better without hearing traffic all night. Remember your earplugs and use them!

Most dirt roads or trails on public land will lead to a 'stealth' camping spot. Try to get behind trees, brush, hills or a mountain. You want to be concealed, along with your fire or candlelight.

Be certain to keep your tent 25 feet away from fire. Ashes will burn through the nylon in seconds. Place your tent on high ground, so that if it rains, you won't wake up feeling like you're being swept over Niagara Falls. Special note: eight out of ten persons reading this advice will choose to learn this lesson the hard way! Trust me, you will wake up in the middle of the night wishing you sported gills!

MAKE CAMP IN PRIMITIVE AREAS

- Secure food and 1.5 gallons of water two or three hours before dusk.
- Look for an abandoned road or trail and 'vanish' into the landscape.
- Pitch your tent on high ground. The sight should be safe from lightning and potential washout from a rainstorm.
- Roll out your air mattress and sleeping bag.
- Place all your gear in exact same place every night.
- Place your miner's lamp near your headrest. Once your tent and gear are secured inside, either lock your bike to a tree or run the cable from the bike to your helmet inside your tent.
- If you have a campfire, make sure it is 25 feet away from your tent. If that is not possible, use your stove for cooking.
- Spread your tablecloth on the ground outside your tent. Tablecloth can be a yard square of plastic.
- Secure your candle lantern where you can use it.
- Organize all your cooking gear and food in front of you.
- If you are using a stove, make sure it's stable. You don't need a scalding injury while away from medical help.
- If you drink coffee, hot chocolate or tea, boil your water first.
- Prepare food. Cook food. Eat like a ravenous wild maniac!
- Wash dishes and clean up all traces of food.
- Always leave the bottom zipper of your tent open if you leave camp to take a bath or for any other reason. Whether you have food in the tent or not, curious squirrels or chipmunks may bite their way through the nylon to see what's inside.

BUILDING CAMPFIRES SAFELY IN THE WILDERNESS

If you enjoy ashes in your soup and burning embers in your potatoes, make yourself happy—cook on an open fire! It's SO romantic and mountain-manish! It's primordial! Humans have enjoyed campfires before the wheel they invented the wheel. It beats watching television, unless you think watching the latest episode of "American Idol" gives meaning to life!

You need to remember a few points about making a fire to keep it safe and under control:

- Always check for, and obey, no-burn rules. Use common sense when camping in a dry area.
- Build a protective rock ring around the fire. You can wet the ground around the fire ring if you have ample water.
- Keep the fire away from tents and other fabrics. Watch out for your Lycra or Gore-Tex. One flying ember will burn a hole in it.
- Keep your eyes on the fire at all times.
- Build the fire away from overhanging tree branches or dry brush. If you build under some low-hanging branches, you might turn the tree into a bonfire. Explain that to the local fire department chief after you've taken her away from her husband and two kids at suppertime. On second thought, maybe she would mind a little adventure away from hubby and the kids…! Finally, avoid building a fire against a large rock or cliff because it will leave unsightly smoke scars.
- Keep a water supply handy in case you need to douse the flames.
- Let the fire burn down before you place your pots in the embers. You want a slow, even heat on your food.
- If it's windy, eat pork and beans out of a can, or a sandwich, or energy bars. Avoid the chance of a runaway fire.
- Before hitting the sack, be certain to put the fire COMPLETELY OUT by smothering it with water or dirt. If you fail to put it out completely, you could cost people their lives and homes. Put that fire out COMPLETELY!
- When finished with the fireplace, spread the rocks out and return the fire area to its natural appearance. Spread the ashes and place

leaves and brush over the fire pit. Really give nature a chance by keeping the wild beautiful. "Leave no trace!"

FIRE IN YOUR TENT

On those rainy or windy days, your first inclination might be to cook in your tent. Don't!

Okay, I know you're starving to death and you hunger for a Big Mac, or Chipotle's Special or a Giant pizza. Again, don't cook in your tent!

There are so many little things that can, and will go wrong when you have an open flame burning in your tent. I'm as careful as a person can be, but once, I nearly turned my tent into a bonfire! Avoid learning this lesson the hard way.

CANDLE LANTERN

The only flame, and I haven't done it in a long time because of miner's lamps with LEDs, is a glass and aluminum-encased candle lantern. Even then, I never leave it in the tent unattended. Make sure it's either hanging from the roof on a string, or resting on a flat surface such as a notepad or book.

Fire inside your tent is nothing to fool with, and that's not a lesson you want to learn the hard way!

SANITATION AND HUMAN WASTE IN THE WILDERNESS

It's very important to follow a few rules when camping in primitive wilderness situations:

When washing dishes, heat the water and use bio-degradable soap. If you're washing in a lake or stream, make sure you discard the soapy water onto the soil at least 15 feet away from the lake or stream water so it drains into the soil. Rinse your cooking gear thoroughly.

Pack out what you pack in! I pick up trash of careless campers. I honor

Mother Nature by leaving a place cleaner than I found it. In the immortal words of the great philosopher Goethe, "Do not think that you can do so little, that you do nothing at all." Avoid burning anything, especially plastic, but do take it in a bag to a proper trash can up in the next town or wherever it's proper and responsible.

Since no toilets are available in primitive campsites, please follow strict wilderness rules:

- Find a spot 20 to 30 yards away from your campsite and away from a water source.
- Dig a hole four to six inches deep. Do your business. Cover your waste with soil. If that is not possible, cover with a rock or leaves. Carry your TP in a 1-gallon zip lock plastic bag and another 1-gallon zip lock bag inside it. Roll your 'soiled' TP into a ball with new TP and place it in the second zip lock bag. No, you don't have to touch the soiled TP. Again, "Leave No Trace!"
- You may burn your used toilet paper in the campfire. If dry conditions exist or combustibles are present, just carry the used TP in the zip lock bag and toss used TP at the next proper disposal.
- In Chile, my friend Doug nearly burned an entire wheat field because the flame he used to burn his toilet paper ignited to the dry stalks. The next thing I knew, Doug waddled toward me with his shorts around his knees, screaming, "I just crapped in the wrong place!" We grabbed six water bottles and ran back to the fire, squirting it with our tiny water guns. A passing motorist and an old lady stopped to help us. You can imagine her shock and confusion when she saw Doug with his shorts at his ankles and me screaming and squirting at the flames. She didn't know whether to help us or faint. Moral of this episode: be careful where you strike a match to your toilet paper—and pull up your pants before you light it!
- Also, clean your hands with 'hand sanitization' or soap and water, or at least rinse your hands.

CLEANING AND HYGIENE

While on tour or any adventure, you're living at a basic level. You're closer to being an animal than you've ever been. Bugs will try to invade your tent and mosquitoes will buzz around your head. Spiders will spin webs across your tent at night and they will be eating their 'catch' when you step out the next day. "You'll go to sleep under moonlight and wake up with the sun. The morning alarm clock might be the laughing call of an Australian kookaburra bird. It's natural, but it's dirty out there on a bike, or backpacking, or mountain climbing or any extended outdoor activity.

That's why you must maintain good sanitation and hygiene practices.

Wash your hands before preparing food. Be certain to use bio-degradable soap in the wilderness. If you don't have any, use any soap or hand cleaner, but make sure you use it. Avoid throwing soapy water into a stream or lake. Throw it onto the land where it can drain into the soil.

After any use of pots and pans, make certain to wash and rinse them. Use your camp towel to wipe them or let them dry in the sun. Please honor Mother Nature and she will bless you with wonders around the next bend in the road or turn of the river.

BEAR AND LION COUNTRY

"Bears are made of the same dust as we, and breathe the same winds and drink of the same waters. A bear's days are warmed by the same sun, his dwellings are over-domed by the same blue sky, and his life turns and ebbs with the heart pulsing like ours. He was poured from the same fountain. And whether he at last goes to our stingy Heave or not, he has terrestrial immortality. His life, not long, not short, knows no beginning, no ending. To him life unstinted, unplanned, is above accidents of time, and his years, markless and boundless, equal eternity," John Muir, hiking in Yosemite Valley, California, 1888

CAMPING IN GRIZZLY, BLACK BEAR AND MOUNTAIN LION COUNTRY

The grizzly is North America's symbol of wilderness. His domain reaches from Yellowstone to Alaska. To catch a glimpse of this great animals fills your eyes with wonder. His wildness defines the wilderness. He remains "king" in his domain.

Nothing will scare the daylights out of you faster than coming face to face with a bear. Few animals will kill you faster than a grizzly if she feels threatened. If she comes in the night, you will feel terror like never before because you have the added uncertainty of darkness. The sound of her grunting will drive your heart into a pumping frenzy, and your blood will race around your body like a Formula One race car at the Indy 500.

I shivered in my sleeping bag while a grizzly dragged his muzzle across the side of my tent one morning in Alaska. His saliva left a mark on the nylon for a few weeks, and a mark for a lifetime on my mind. I'll never forget the three-and-a-half-inch claws that tore through the back of my tent...that day. I lucked out!

Bears prove capricious, unpredictable and dangerous. They search for food 24/7. Anything that looks edible to them makes for fair game. They eat berries, salmon, moose, deer, mice and humans without discrimination.

That's why this section deals with camping in grizzly bear, black bear and mountain lion country.

If you travel, hike and camp in remote regions of North America, or other areas of the world, sooner or later, you will camp in bear country. It's not something to be feared, but it is something you must respect. You are in his dining room.

The key to your safety and survival in Mr. Grizzly's domain: respect! You must honor the rules of the wilderness. You must follow those rules each and every time you camp, hike or otherwise make your way into his territory. You may not get a second chance.

Imagine looking into a grizzly's eyes, backed by his 800 pounds of teeth and claws, and pleading, "Gee, Mr. Bear, could you give me a break this time...I'm really story I left my chocolate chip cookies inside my tent...can we make a deal, like, I'll give you my first-born child...please, pretty please...."

Never assume a bear won't walk into your life.

At the same time, you cannot camp in fear. During my many journeys to Alaska, I enjoyed extraordinary moments watching rogue grizzlies fishing for salmon and mother grizzlies playing with their cubs. Great wonder and amazing moments!

I also had the living hell scared out of me because of my own carelessness.

By using common sense and following the rules, you can minimize the chances and danger of a bear confrontation. But your safety cannot be guaranteed. You could do everything right, and still run into a bear—especially if he's trying to find food for his evening dinner!

However, since I've alarmed you, let me put this in proper perspective! Former Governor Sarah Palin lives in Alaska, and she alleges she has outrun a few grizzly bears. Therefore, if you're camping with Sarah, the only thing you have to do: run faster than her!

If you follow nature's rules, your chances of a bear confrontation are less than a lightning strike. Therefore, go ahead and enjoy yourself. And if you do encounter a bear, you will return home with great bear stories that will keep your friends glued to your every word.

Remember: food and food odors attract bears, which makes them overcome their fear of humans. Be smart and keep food odor off your body and ten, and away from your camping site.

RULES FOR CAMPING IN BEAR COUNTRY

Camp in an area least likely to be visited by bears. Stay away from animal trails, large droppings, diggings, berry bushes, beehives and watering holes. Don't swim in streams where salmon run. If you do, you may end up running for your own life.

Make absolutely certain your tent has no food odor in or on it. If you have spilled jam or peanut butter, grizzlies especially like Skippy's Crunch Style, on your tent fabric, wash it clean.

Cook 300 feet away from your tent. Wash your gear thoroughly. Do not sleep in the same clothes that you wore while eating and cooking dinner.

Make sure you avoid keeping perfume, deodorant or toothpaste in your tent. Keep anything that has an odor in your food bag and hang it away from your camp.

Hang your food in a strong 1.5-millimeter-thick plastic bag at least 300 feet from your tent. That means your camp, cooking and food hanging areas are in a triangle, 300 feet apart. If a bear does amble into your sector, he will go after your food bag, and more than likely, he won't bother you.

Bear-proof canisters that can carry several days of food supplies cost about $100.00 and can be purchased at most camping outlets mentioned in this book. www.REI.com

After you have hung your food, take out a wet cloth and wipe your face and hands to ensure you have no food odor on them.

Finally, brush and floss your teeth. You wouldn't want a tiny piece of food between your molars to be the reason you inadvertently invited Mr. Grizz to feast upon your tenderloin body at night. Can you imagine the coroner's report in Whitehorse, Yukon, "Gourmet camper was mauled last night because he left one little piece of fried chicken between his teeth... he could have starred in the movie "Dumb and Dumber.""

Also, remember to employ the same sanitation rules you learned in the primitive camping section.

Hanging food: Attach one end of a parachute cord to a rock or carabineer and throw it over a tree limb. Use the other end of the cord to tie your food bag. Pull the bag into the air at least 12 feet above the ground, at least five feet from the tree trunk and at least five feet from the limb where the cord is hanging. Secure the parachute cord by tying it to a limb at the base of the tree or some other tree.

A second method for hanging food: Loop two bags over a limb so they balance each other and let them dangle with no tie-off cord. Some bears have figured out to follow the tie-off cord and release it by batting or pawing it—mostly in Yellowstone where so many careless campers visit. This second method should discourage a bear's efforts. Again, keep it 12 feet off the round, at least five feet away from tree trunk.

A third method: throw a line over the branches of two trees about ten feet apart. Throw the same parachute cord over the line and hang your food bag between the trees on the line. Do what works best for you.

Grizzlies do not intentionally prey on humans. As long as they are not drawn to any food odor, you should enjoy a good night's sleep.

IF A BEAR OR MOUNTAIN LION SHOULD CONFRONT YOU

Okay, you've followed the rules, but you wake up to the sounds of a bear outside your tent, or something else that's breathing and prowling through the night mist. Your nostrils fill with the stench of something that's got a really bad case of body odor.

You don't carry a gun, but you do have your Swiss Army knife! Yeah, great! The bear would snatch it out of your hands and use it for a toothpick afterwards! If you did carry a gun, it would only piss him off! But you kept your bear repellant spray right next to your sleeping bag, so you pull it out. Yes, bear spray will stop a grizzly better than a gun.

At that moment, you wish you could sprint like an NFL halfback or fly like an eagle!

What to do: Stay calm. Remember that bears and mountain lions don't like humans. It could be a deer, moose or elk. Unless you're in bear country in early spring, when a bear is just out of his den and hungry, he may only be curious and sniffing around.

I have been told that a good strategy is to play dead inside your sleeping bag if you're attacked by a grizzly. If you're with another person, you may opt to run in different directions. At least one of you would live! Keep that bear spray in your hand! No hard and fast rules exist that guarantee anything in this situation.

During the day, be alert. If you come in contact with a grizzly, try to move out his area. Never run! Make a lot of noise by blowing on a whistle if you're hiking. If a bear sees you and charges, turn sideways and do not look at him directly, but do point your bear spray at his face. He may still attack you, but then again, if you are not threatening, he may not. If he continues charging to within 30 feet, spray a stream of bear spray at his nose, and follow the stream with your own eyes until you hit him right on the nose and continue the stream. It will stop him. Make sure your friend carries a second can of spray to continue the point-blank spraying if needed. Some folks carry wasp & hornet spray for backup.

If you don't have bear spray, shame on you, but if the attack continues, drop to the ground and assume the cannonball position with your hands over your head to protect your head and stomach.

If you run, he mostly like will chase you down. At this juncture, you may want to…cry, pray, scream or faint. It may not do any good, but it may make you feel better. If your prayer isn't working, make a quick conversion to another religion and pray faster. If you die, you died while on a great adventure, which makes it a bit heroic. It's better to die this way than suffering a heart attacks while eating chocolate bon- bons on a Barker Lounger in front of an NFL game with the remote glued to your hand.

Black bears: when confronting black bears, you have a much better chance of survival. Stand your ground. Do not drop to the ground or play dead. Don't look into his eyes; stay on your feet and keep that bear spray pointed right at his nose. Don't look scared, even if you're wetting your pants with fear. Maintain your composure until the black bear leaves your area. Practice using the bear spray or hornet spray.

Mountain lion: if confronted with a mountain lion or puma, stand your ground and make yourself appear larger if possible, by spreading out your hands and/or hopping up on a log or rock. Move away slowly and keep the 'bear' spray aimed at the lion. If you have a child with you, pick him or her up and hold the child close to you. With a cat, you can fight back, and it may run away. It also may run if you throw rocks at it. Do not run yourself. Again, it's between you and lady luck.

Adventure is not always comfortable, but it is still adventure. I am a firm believer that neither bliss nor adventure are ever obtained by staying home in your rocking chair.

As a final note, be confident that you will make your way through bear country safely when you follow the rules of Mother Nature. When you respect Mother Nature, she will respect you right back.

I can see you sitting around the table with your friends after your adventure in Alaska:

In your journal, "Yeah, I woke up one morning on the Kenai River when I heard a blood-curdling growl…I thought the sun was shining through my mosquito netting, but it was the pearly whites of a 900 pound grizzly…well sir, I didn't have much time to think, so I pulled out my Bowie Knife—kinda' like Daniel Boone—and stared back into that grizzly's eyes. That's when I gave him a toothy growl of my own. It scared him so badly, he scrambled up a tree, where we used him for an umbrella to keep the 24-hour sun from burning down on us while we ate fresh salmon steaks on the campfire and talked to Alaska Governor Sarah Palin in the next campsite."

Jack London would have been proud!

TENT CAMPING

Release the valve on the air mattress first so it is ready when you get everything inside. A key to camping success is having everything where you want it, when you need it. That means replacing the same gear in the same pouch every single time you use it. ALWAYS zip up a pouch immediately after taking out or putting something into it. Make it a habit.

Before cooking dinner, you might want to take a bath first, before the sun goes down and the air cools. Soap, towel and shower shoes are all you need. If it's a swiftly moving stream, be careful with your bottle of biodegradable soap.

A special note on campfires. Gather your wood before dark. Pick up kindling and larger branches. Stick with dead wood. Be sure the fire pit is a safe distance from your tent. Sparks carry on the breeze and will melt nylon in seconds. Make certain the flames won't catch adjoining grass or overhanging branches on fire. A circular rock firewall is a good safety factor. Place paper and kindling at the bottom. Light the fire, get it going and keep adding larger and larger wood until you have a good flame. If you cook on and open fire, keep your pot in a heavy plastic bag to keep the black soot from smudging your gear. If your campsite is in a dry zone where fire hazards are high, use common sense when building a fire, and decide not to build one, if it's a high wind area. ALWAYS put the fire totally out with water at night and in the morning. Clean the pit and spread the rocks around. Replace twigs and leaves over the pit before you leave.

When you're ready for sleep, use one of your panniers for a pillow and a sweater to make a cushion. Or, purchase and air pillow at a camping store. Be certain to check for mosquitoes by shining your flashlight around the tent. If you see one, kill the devil. Now you're ready for sleep. Or are you? If you are in deep wilderness where bears or other large meat-eating animals live, leave no food in your tent. Put it in a plastic bag and hang it in a tree, 300 feet from your tent. Be certain to brush your teeth, and wash your face and hands so no food odor is on your person. If you have fruit in your tent, and it's touching the floor, ants will cut the nylon in a few hours. Don't give them the chance. Any time you leave camp for a hike, do not leave food in the tent, and leave it open so chipmunks can get in. If they can't, they will chew holes through your tent.

In the morning, you may need to take your daily constitutional. That's fine. Just remember the rules of camping. Bury your feces if possible. As for your toilet paper, burn it, bury it or wrap it up and carry it out to throw away or burn at an appropriate time. When burning it, use prudent judgment in high fire areas of dry grass. It's that simple. In fact, leave the campsite cleaner than you found it. Burn or carry out the trash and put in a proper disposal. No matter how trashed a place is, you don't have to become a part of the problem, you can be a part of the solution.

When breaking camp, pack your gear and clean out the tent. Pull your stakes and count them before dropping in the bag. Do not let them lay on the ground where they can get stepped on. Fold the tent along with ground cloth and place in the stuff sack. You might try changing your folding pattern periodically, so you don't cause premature deterioration on waterproofing and fabric. Strap your gear on the bike. Walk the bike out of the area, and go back to look over everything to see that you have all your gear, including the food bag that hung from the tree. Don't be surprised if you walk up on a bear scratching his head trying to figure out how to get to your food bag.

When you're satisfied that you have everything secured, it's time to pedal. If the camp site was beautiful, you may have taken a few photographs for memories of your home in the woods.

When you follow a solid routine for camping each night, you wake up refreshed and relaxed. Camping goes hand in hand for great wilderness adventures.

DOGS

One last point about dogs chasing you. Always carry an air horn in your handlebar bag or in a location you can grab it in a second. A short blast will frighten them away from you without harming them. Some riders use a small cannister of Mace. Either one will save you from dog bites. Always be aware of them in small towns or along country roads. Most will bark before they get to you, but some will remain silent until their right on your heels. Be alert at all times.

"While bicycle adventure-touring turns from days into weeks and weeks into months, you turn a corner in your mind, your heart and your spirit. You tap into a wellspring of eternal emotional bliss. You push two pedals that give your body renewed energy with every stroke. You see things differently while gaining whole new perspectives. You transform from one person into a whole new individual every day. Ironically, no psychologist can figure it out. But you know! The energy of the universe charges through every cell in your body to create pure enchantment." FHW

About the Author

Frosty Wooldridge, Golden, Colorado, lives each day with gratitude, boundless enthusiasm and a sense of purpose for everything he undertakes. He graduated from Michigan State University. He loves mountain climbing, scuba diving, swing dancing, skiing, tennis, racquetball and bicycle touring. He writes and speaks on overpopulation and environmental challenges facing humanity. He has taught at the elementary, high school and college levels. He has rafted, canoed, backpacked, sailed, windsurfed, snowboarded and more all over the planet. He has bicycled 100,000 miles on six continents and 15 times across the United States. His feature articles have appeared in national and international magazines for 30 years. He has interviewed on NBC, CBS, ABC, CNN, FOX and 100 radio shows. His website contains more information for anyone aspiring toward a spectacular life:

www.HowtoLiveaLifeofAdventure.com

Facebook adventure pages:
How to Live a Life of Adventure: The Art of Exploring the World
Bicycle Touring Unique Moments
Bicycling Poets

Acknowledgements: Special thanks to Sandi Lynn for brilliant copy editing along with ideas for creating a compelling and motivational piece of literature. Thanks to my fabulous wife Sandi for her treasured ideas and daily support.

Book cover: Sandi and Frosty Wooldridge standing by their bikes on the Oregon coast.

Other books by the author:

Handbook for Touring Bicyclists—Bicycling touring grows in popularity each year. Men and women around the world take to the highways and the "open air" is their kitchen. On the pages of this book, you'll discover how to buy, carry, prepare and store food while on tour. Discover the ins and outs with a "Baker's Dozen" of touring tips that are essential for successful bicycle adventuring. Whether you're going on a weekend ride, a weeklong tour or two years around the world, this handbook will help you learn the artistry of bicycling and cooking.

Strike Three! Take Your Base—The Brookfield Reader, Sterling, VA. To order this hardcover book, send $19.95 to Frosty Wooldridge by contacting him through his website. This poignant story is important reading for every teen who has ever experienced the loss of a parent from either death or divorce. This is the story of a boy losing his father and growing through his sense of pain and loss. It is the story of baseball, a game that was shared by both the boy and his father, and how baseball is much like life.

Antarctica: An Extreme Encounter— "This book transports readers into the bowels of million-year-old glaciers, katabatic winds, to the tops of smoking volcanoes, scuba diving under the ice, intriguing people, death, outlaw activities and rare moments where the author meets penguins, whales, seals and Skua birds. Hang on to your seat belts. You're in for a wild ride where the bolt goes into the bottom of the world." Sandy Colhoun

Bicycling Around the World: Tire Tracks for your Imagination—This book mesmerizes readers with animal stories that bring a smile to your face. It chills you with a once-in-a-lifetime ride in Antarctica where you'll meet a family of Emperor penguins. Along the way, you'll find out that you have to go without a mirror, sometimes, in order to see yourself. The greatest aspect of this book comes from—expectation. Not since **Miles from Nowhere** has a writer captured the Zen and Art of Bicycle Adventure as well as Wooldridge. Not only that, you may enjoy a final section: "Everything you need to know about long distance touring." He shows you "How to live the dream." You will possess the right bike, equipment, money and tools to ride into your own long-distance touring adventures. If you like bicycling, you'll go wild reading this book. If you don't like bicycling, you'll still go wild reading this book.

Motorcycle Adventure to Alaska: Into the Wind— "Seldom does a book capture the fantasy and reality of an epic journey the magnitude of this book. Trevor and Dan resemble another duo rich in America's history of youthful explorers who get into all kinds of trouble—Tom Sawyer and Huckleberry Finn. They plied the Mississippi River, but Dan and his brother push their machines into a wild and savage land—Alaska. My boys loved it." John Mathews, father of two boys and a daughter.

Bicycling the Continental Divide: Slice of Heaven, Taste of Hell— "This bicycle dream ride carries a bit of mountain man adventure. The author mixes hope with frustration, pain with courage and bicycling over the mountains. John Brown, a friend left behind to battle cancer, provides guts and heart for his two friends who ride into the teeth of nature's fury. Along the way, you'll laugh, cry and gain new appreciations while pondering the meaning of life." Paul Jackson

Losing Your Best Friend: Vacancies of the Heart— "This is one heck of a powerful book. It's a must read for anyone that has lost a friend or parent. It will give you answers that you may not have thought about. It will touch your heart and you will learn from their experiences. It also shows you what you can do if you suffer conflict with your friend's wife or girlfriend." Jonathan Runy

Rafting the Rolling Thunder— "Fasten your raft-belts folks. You're in for the white-water rafting ride of your life. Wooldridge keeps readers on the edge of their seats on a wild excursion through the Grand Canyon. Along the way, he offers you an outlaw-run by intrepid legend "High Water Harry," a man who makes a bet with the devil and nearly loses his life. The raft bucks beneath you as Harry crashes through Class V rapids. And the Grand Canyon Dish Fairies, well, they take you on separate rides of laughter and miles of smiles. Enjoy this untamed excursion on a river through time." Jason Rogers

Misty's Long Ride: Across America on Horseback—by Howard Wooldridge (Frosty Wooldridge's brother). "As good as Howard was, sometimes there was nothing he could do about our situation in the burning inferno of Utah. In that agonizing desert, a man's mouth became so dry, he couldn't spit. I felt the heat cook my hooves at ground level where it felt like walking alone in the middle of a farrier's furnace. Above us, vultures soared in the skies searching for roadkill. Yet, Howard pulled down the brim of his hat and pushed forward. I followed this cowboy because he was a Long Rider and I was his horse." For anyone who loves horses and high adventure, Howard's horse Misty tells one of the great adventure tales in the 21st century by galloping across America. You'll enjoy horse sense, horse humor, unique characters and ride across America.

How to Deal with 21st Century Women: Co-Creating a Successful Relationship— "The chapters on the nine key points for creating a successful long-term relationship are the best suggestions for anyone considering marriage. Every woman should read them along with her man. This is the first male relationship book that honors the male perspective and aims for sensible collaboration. I highly recommend this book for men and women." Chelsea Robinson

How to Live a Life of Adventure: The Art of Exploring the World— "If you endeavor to live like you mean it, to aspire to show up with passion and purpose, and take your being to maximum heart rate in mind and body—please allow Frosty to coach, inspire and guide you. *How to Live a Life of Adventure* will rock your body and soul, and enliven within you your belief and practice of living like you mean it—with passion and purpose." James Rouse

America on the Brink: The Next Added 100 Million Americans— Electrifying reading! This is a veritable cannonade of a book. Wooldridge targets the people and institutions, from the president of the USA on down, who refuse to look at the consequences of population growth in the modern era. His focus is on the United States, but his range is the world. He fearlessly addresses issues that politicians fear to mention, such as the effects of mass immigration on our population future and social systems. He engages leaders to force population issues into our local and national political decisions. Lindsey Grant, former Deputy Assistant Secretary of State for Environment and Population.

Living Your Spectacular Life— "This book entertains, inspires and motivates. What I liked most about it: Wooldridge offers other motivational writers in each chapter to give you new ideas on living a spectacular life. He wants you to succeed for your sake. If that means you enjoy a greater affinity to another writer, he gives you plenty of choices. He's got six concepts and six practices that provide you with personal courage, self-confidence and empowerment. He offers you dozens of ordinary men and women living spectacular lives in various pursuits from world travel to growing a garden. He kept me reading through every chapter." Jake Hodges

Old Men Bicycling Across America: A Journey Beyond Old Age— "This book is a ton of fun. Five gray-haired, bald and grizzled old guys get together around a campfire along with one of them a guitarist, and they sing and tell stories. If you can imagine that all of them had been married one, two and three times, well, their stories lifted into the treetops with outrageous laughter. More than that, they followed the Lewis & Clark Trail all the way to Bismarck, North Dakota on the northern tier bicycle route, the longest ride in America. This book will make you want to take the ride yourself." Rex Hamilton

All books available at: 1 888 519 5121, www.amazon.com, www.barnesandnoble.com, also on Kindle.

Praise for: **Zen Between Two Bicycle Wheels—Eat, Pedal, Sleep Baby Boomers Bicycling The West Coast**

"Say what you will about these two old people, but they possess the hearts of lions. This book surprised me. I'm a female baby boomer who loves to ride my bicycle, but I had no idea that a 70-year-old woman can ride nearly 2,000 miles down the West Coast. It seemed too daunting, but Sandi made it happen. She's got tons of gumption. She advised to, 'Just keep pedaling one day at a time and you will find yourself in the middle of your own dream.' She's living it for real. If you're a doubting baby boomer, this book will carry you into a whole new realm of your own possibilities. This is a fun read." June Lockart

"Can't say as I could ever ride my bicycle down the West Coast, but I really enjoyed his 'well-told' story, his inspiring quotes and his superb pictures. I have been riding a bicycle since the 1950's, so I know the feeling. The author gave me a sense of riding alongside of him and his wife. I'd highly recommend this book to young and old, alike." Gerald Johnson

"Whether you're young or old, you will enjoy the 'high energy' of this book. I read the biography of the author. He's bicycled across six continents and 15 times across the USA. That's beyond my physical paygrade. But after reading this book, I'm only 66 and I would like to bicycle the West Coast. He's got a whole chapter that shows you everything you need to make the ride yourself. He's pretty unique for an old timer. Read this book! It's fun!" Charles Johnson

"I've never seen the redwoods. I've never driven along the coast of Oregon. I've never seen Big Sur. I've never crossed the Golden Gate Bridge. I don't even own a bicycle. But after reading this book, I want to do everything Sandi and Frosty did. I am so inspired after reading about their travels. I especially liked the "astonishing" episodes of Frosty's travels around the world at the end of the book. I was deeply touched by the inspiring narrative in this book." Richard Wolcott

"Read this book! It's a hoot! The author guides you down the West Coast with his lovely wife. I was inspired by their relationship on this journey.

They may be two old people, yet they enjoy a sense of adventure of a young couple. For anyone enjoying their "Golden Years" whether by auto travel or bicycle or armchair adventure, this book gives a refreshing outlook on life. I highly recommend it." John Lambert

"This is an enormous book for female baby boomers. It gently shows you, that you too, can make a bicycle ride down the West Coast or across Europe. With the information on touring, along with touring companies, you can choose your favorite style of exploration. I really liked the wisdom of this book. There's no doubt the author learned a lot about the world during his travels. Sandi gave me courage to get into shape and ride myself. I've always wanted to make such a bicycle tour. As a former English teacher, I can say the author exhibited eloquent writing. Now I have the courage to try it." Margaret Tinsdale

"I really liked the 'epic moments' at the end of the book. The author recounted some of his most harrowing and sublime experiences while touring around the world. Most of all, I liked his conversational style that kept me turning the pages. The photographs gave me a sense of riding along with them. I highly recommend this book for cyclists of all ages." Paula McIntyre

"If this book doesn't get you off your keyster, nothing will! This book could be billed as the 'Zen of Bicycling' because he brings a lifetime of travel knowledge. I liked this one statement the most, "The long-distance bicyclist carries an insatiable desire to interact with possibilities that may emerge around the next bend in the road. His or her curiosity drives the pedals that turn the wheels. Each cyclist carries a sense of "stubborn joy" into the day. The bicyclist lives in that moment and then pedals forward to the next moment, always advancing, never in retreat." That says it all. I've already visited my bike store to inquire about a touring bike." Robert H. Dafoe.

The End